THE PRACTICE OF
EMOTIONALLY FOCUSED
MARITAL THERAPY

CREATING
CONNECTION

BRUNNER/MAZEL
BASIC PRINCIPLES INTO PRACTICE SERIES
Series Editor: Natalie H. Gilman

The *Brunner/Mazel Basic Principles Into Practice Series* is designed to present—in a series of concisely written, easily understandable volumes—the basic theory and clinical principles associated with a variety of disciplines and types of therapy. These volumes will serve not only as "refreshers" for practicing therapists, but also as basic texts on the college and graduate level.

BRUNNER/MAZEL
BASIC PRINCIPLES INTO PRACTICE SERIES
VOLUME 11

THE PRACTICE OF EMOTIONALLY FOCUSED MARITAL THERAPY

CREATING CONNECTION

SUSAN M. JOHNSON, ED.D.

BRUNNER/MAZEL, *A member of the Taylor & Francis Group*

Library of Congress Cataloging-in-Publication Data

Johnson, Susan M.
The practice of emotionally focused marital therapy:
   creating connection/Susan M. Johnson.
        p. cm. — (Brunner/Mazel basic principles into practice
series; v. 11)
     Includes bibliographical references and index.
     ISBN 0-87630-817-5 (pbk.)
     1. Marital psychotherapy. I. Title. II. Series.
RC488.5.J59 1996
616.89′156—dc20   96-31146
                                                              CIP

Published by
Brunner/Mazel
A member of the Taylor & Francis Group
325 Chestnut Street, Suite 800
Philadelphia, PA 19106

Manufactured in the United States of America
        10   9   8   7   6   5

*This book is dedicated to my partner, John Palmer Douglas,
my secure base and the love of my life.*

CONTENTS

FOREWORD

As I sat down to write this foreword, words came with great difficulty. I asked myself why had Susan Johnson asked me to say anything in the first place? Then, at once, I flashed on an editorial I had written 10 years earlier, when I was the editor of the *Journal of Marital and Family Therapy.* The title of that editorial was, "A Time for Connections." With that in mind, I instantly knew why she had invited me. We were kindred clinicians, seeking to break down artificial and dangerous boundaries.

There are important boundaries *The Practice of Emotionally Focused Marital Therapy: Creating Connection* successfully crosses. The first, and most obvious, boundary is whatever separates the members of a couple therapy emotionally. Now, focusing on closing this gap may not seem to constitute a particularly striking breakthrough for clinical practice, but look again. For most of the last two decades, what many of us have considered to be "advances" in couple therapy has involved such therapeutic maneuvers as exhorting mates to trade discrete desirable behaviors, instructing them to pretend to have certain interactional problems, and asking about overnight miracle changes as though doing so would bring about miracles overnight.

Lo and behold, we seem to have forgotten that people usually make long-term intimate commitments because they love each other, need each other, and find their connection to be the most important relationship they think they'll ever have with anyone. Is this mushy nonsense? No, it's real life. And it is in these real-life, real-time terms that Susan Johnson pushes us to work with couples in therapy. This partner–partner connection is ultimately what couple therapy is all about. Sure, some of the above-mentioned techniques can facilitate important changes in couple interaction, but do interactional changes necessarily lead to connection at the gut experiential level? No, not necessarily. Although, focusing on the emotions involved in a couple's interactions may seem an obvious thing to do, it is not what many of us have been doing. So, Dr. Johnson's clear demonstrations of how to reintroduce emotion into the interactional field does, indeed, qualify as a clinical breakthrough.

In a related vein, she asks us to help relationship partners get reconnected to themselves. Emotionally Focused Therapy addresses the "split-off," the anxiety-laden, the unacceptable within ourselves, without the usual kinds of psycho-jargon that so insidiously pathologizes perfectly normal and understandable human behavior. Many family and couple therapists have shown that inner experience can be shifted by behavioral and structural changes in family interactions. Dr. Johnson reminds us persuasively that patterns of interaction can likewise be changed by facilitating change in a couple's inner experience. Some methods of therapy are better at producing internal change, and some are better at producing external change, but it is probably true that all effective therapies help produce change at multiple levels of human experience. Dr. Johnson reawakens our awareness to the fact that significant change in couple therapy can come about by individually focused, yet contextually sensitive clinical methods that, for far too long, have been discounted and demeaned in the field of family and couple therapy.

If *The Practice of Emotionally Focused Marital Therapy: Creating Connection* reflects where the field of couple therapy is going, then perhaps it signals the return to the realm of psychotherapeutic sanity, in which people are dealt with not as cybernetic systems or containers of perverse strivings, but as people. If I am being too optimistic, and this is not where the field is currently headed, then perhaps *The Practice of Emotionally Focused Marital Therapy: Creating Connection* will help to lead us there.

Alan S. Gurman, Ph.D.
Professor of Psychiatry
University of Wisconsin Medical School

ACKNOWLEDGMENTS

First and foremost, I would like to acknowledge the couples and families who have shared themselves and their lives with me over the years. As they have struggled and grown, so they have touched and taught me about human frailty and strength, including my own, and about the mystery we all strive to understand—the creation of secure connectedness with those closest to us. I am honored to have been part of their struggle.

I also gratefully acknowledge the input of my colleague and coauthor, Dr. Les Greenberg, whose seminal work on emotion and experiential psychotherapy has encouraged and informed me.

I would also like to thank Ms. Margorie Clegg and Ms. Lynn Williams-Keeler for their editing of this manuscript.

I would also like to acknowledge the support and creative input of my clinic team at the Ottawa Civic Hospital and my students at the University of Ottawa, whose love of learning and deep respect for the families and couples they see constantly renew my own passion for, and commitment to, this work.

THE PRACTICE OF
EMOTIONALLY FOCUSED
MARITAL THERAPY

CREATING
CONNECTION

1

MARITAL THERAPY AND EFT

In the Book of Proverbs, the "way of a man with a maiden" is identified as one of the great mysteries of the world. In our own century, the task of how to create and maintain a fulfilling, loving relationship with a mate is still considered by many to be a mysterious and daunting undertaking. The marital therapist accompanies his/her clients as they struggle with this mystery. Until recently, the marital therapist made this journey without the guidance of clinical, theoretical, and research road-maps. Such maps have however, in the last decade, dramatically changed the field of marital therapy and enhanced our understanding of marital distress, the process of change, and the nature of adult attachment. This book outlines the practice of Emotionally Focused Marital Therapy (EFT), an approach that uses these new maps to chart a specific course from marital discord to secure connectedness.

In general, marital therapists in the 90s can be clear about the essential nature of marital distress; it is no longer so mysterious. It is about being flooded by negative emotions and trapped in narrow, constricting interactions (Gottman, 1994). These therapists can also find in the marital therapy literature clearly specified technologies for change, in the form of empirically validated treatment interventions; (Greenberg & Johnson, 1988; Jacobson & Margolin, 1979; Snyder & Wills, 1989). They can read the new literature that now exists on the nature of adult love (Hazan & Shaver, 1994; Sternberg & Barnes,

1

1988), a phenomenon that has been somewhat neglected in the marital therapy field (Roberts, 1992). In addition, new elaborations on important aspects of change in marital therapy, such as the role of emotion in the therapy process, are also available (Johnson & Greenberg, 1994).

Marital therapy as a discipline seems to be coming of age. Its application is also widening, and it is now used to address more and more "individual" symptomatology (Jacobson, Holtzworth-Munroe, & Schmaling, 1989). This makes sense in the light of recent research that links the quality of intimate relationships and social support to individual physical and psychological health through mechanisms such as effective immune system functioning and the amelioration of life stress and trauma (Burman & Margolin, 1992; Kiecolt-Glaser et al., 1987; Pennebaker, 1990).

THE EMERGENCE OF EFT

EFT was formulated in the early 1980s (Greenberg & Johnson, 1988; Johnson & Greenberg, 1985) as a response to the lack of clearly delineated and validated marital interventions, particularly more humanistic and less behavioral interventions. It was called EFT to draw attention to emotion as a powerful agent of change, rather than as simply part of the problem of marital distress. The essence of EFT is that it helps distressed partners reprocess their emotional responses so that they can interact in new ways. At the same time, it also shapes interactions that then evoke corrective emotional experiences.

This focus on the positive use of emotion in marital therapy was not part of the established literature in the 1980s. Until recently, emotion has been viewed as a secondary complication arising during the course of behavior and/or cognition, as a disruptive force in therapy, or as simply an inefficient agent of change (Jacobson & Margolin, 1979). It was always clear to marital therapists that changes in affect were a necessary part of relationship repair, but such changes were presumed to arise through cognitive and behavioral means. In the

1990s, the compelling role of emotion in marital distress and the need to explicitly address emotion in marital therapy has become much more accepted (Gottman, 1994; Johnson & Greenberg, 1994).

At this point in time, there are seven studies in existence showing favorable treatment outcomes for EFT with different populations (Johnson, Greenberg, & Schlindler, 1996), and several studies delineating the therapy process and change events (Greenberg et al., 1993; Johnson & Greenberg, 1988), as well as one study of predictors of success in EFT (Johnson & Talitman, in press). The effects of EFT have also been compared favorably with those of other approaches (Dunn & Schwebel, 1995; Johnson & Greenberg, 1985).

There are, therefore, some answers to the four key questions for any intervention, namely: Does it work? Does it work relative to other approaches? How does it work—that is, what has to happen in the therapy process to create change? and Whom does it work for—that is, what kinds of couples, with what kinds of problems are particularly suited to EFT?

At the same time research into the effects of EFT interventions was being conducted, the theoretical conceptualization underlying EFT was also developing. From the beginning, EFT focused on the relationship between partners in terms of an emotional bond, rather than a bargain to be renegotiated. However, the relevance of attachment theory (Bowlby, 1969, 1988) has become more and more apparent, as EFT interventions have been refined and the process of change has become clearer (Johnson & Greenberg, 1995). Social psychologists also began to contribute to the study of love and now clearly identify attachment theory as the most promising perspective on adult love relationships (Hazan & Shaver, 1987). Thus, attachment theory has become more and more a part of EFT.

At this point, EFT is the most empirically validated approach to marital therapy, apart from the behavioral approaches (Alexander, Holtzworth-Munroe, & Jameson, 1994), and the need for a book outlining this approach from a pragmatic clinical point of view became apparent. The purpose of this book is to teach clinicians how to implement EFT in as systematic a way as possible, given the uniqueness of every couple and every relationship, and the intricacies of the therapy process. Theory is included only where necessary to provide the lens through which the EFT therapist views marital distress and the process of change in marital therapy.

The strengths of EFT are:

- Its assumptions, strategies, and interventions are clearly specified and delineated. It is replicable and has been used to train numerous practicing marital therapists.
- There is substantial empirical support for its effectiveness with general and specific populations, for example, with parents of chronically ill children (Walker, Johnson, Manion, Cloutier, in press) and it is associated with relatively large treatment effects (Johnson et al., 1996). It has also given rise to research on the process of therapy and on client variables associated with treatment success, which allows therapists to begin to match clients to treatment.
- The process of the couple's journey through therapy is outlined in nine steps, which are described later in the chapter.
- This approach is grounded in a clear theoretical base. This base consists of a theory of change, which arises from a synthesis of humanistic experiential therapy and systems theory and a theory of adult love, which is viewed as an attachment process.
- The formulation of EFT is extremely congruent with recent empirical studies on the nature of marital distress, which focus on rigid interactional patterns, compelling negative affect, and the nature of adult attachment.

In a climate of dwindling resources for mental health services and managed care, EFT has the advantage of being a structured short-term, empirically validated treatment. In most EFT outcome studies, effective treatment has consisted of 10 to 12 sessions. It is the authors' clinical impression that focusing explicitly on attachment processes, using "new" emotional responses to shape interactional positions, and creating powerful bonding events in the session enables the EFT therapist to be effective in a relatively short time.

WHAT IS THE EFT APPROACH?

EFT looks within and between. It integrates an *intrapsychic* focus on how individuals process their experience, particularly their emotional responses, with an *interpersonal* focus on how partners organize their interactions into patterns and cycles. The process of experiencing and the process of interacting are touchstones for the therapist, as he or she attempts to guide the distressed couple from negative and rigidly structured internal and external responses toward the sensitive responsiveness that is the basis of a secure bond between intimates. Interactional positions are assumed to be maintained by both the partner's emotional experience and the way interactions are organized, that is by intrapsychic realities and the rules of the relationship. These realities and rules are reciprocally determining and constantly recreate each other. Both have to be reprocessed and reorganized, if the couple are to attain a positive emotional bond. The creation of such a bond is the ultimate goal of EFT.

EFT expands experience and interactions. The first goal of therapy is to access and reprocess the emotional responses underlying each partner's interactional position, thereby facilitating a shift in these positions towards accessibility and responsiveness, the building blocks of secure bonds. The second goal of therapy is to create new interactional events that redefine the relationship as a source of security and comfort for each of the partners. The reprocessing of inner experience is used to expand the interpersonal context (a partner discovers that his wife is desperate rather than malicious). In turn, the structuring of new interactional events expands and redefines each partner's inner experience (a spouse expresses his need for his wife, and she then experiences her own fear of responding, rather than focusing on his unavailability).

When EFT is successfully implemented, each partner experiences the other as a source of security, protection, and comfort. Each partner can then assist the other in regulating negative affect and constructing a positive and potent sense of self. The EFT therapist also creates bonding events/interactions in the session, which redefine the relationship.

This process is a journey.

- from alienation to emotional engagement;
- from vigilant defense and self-protection to openness and risk taking;
- from a passive helplessness in the face of the inexorable dance of the relationship to a sense of being able to actively create that dance;
- from desperate blaming of the other to a sense of how each partner makes it difficult for the other to be responsive and caring;
- from a focus on the other's flaws to the discovery of one's own fears and longings;
- but most of all, from isolation to connectedness.

This is not an easy journey for any couple, even with guidance of a seasoned therapist.

As the EFT therapist helps each person expand and reorganize his/her inner experience, the expression of this experience then involves a new presentation of self, a new way of relating to the partner, which in turn evokes new responses from this partner. Stated slightly differently, new experience creates a new kind of dialogue, and this new dialogue creates new interactional events. These events then constitute new steps and initiate new patterns in the couple's dance.

HOW IS EFT DIFFERENT FROM OTHER THERAPEUTIC APPROACHES?

Role of the Therapist

The EFT therapist is not a coach teaching communication skills or more effective ways for partners to negotiate with each other. The EFT therapist is also not a creator of insight into the past and how patterns from one's family of origin might influence one's marriage. In addition, this therapist is not a strategist employing paradox and problem prescription and not a teacher who helps couples modify irrational expectations and beliefs about marriage and relationships.

The EFT therapist is rather a *process consultant*, helping partners to reprocess their experience, particularly their emotional experience of the relationship, as well as a *choreographer*, helping couples to restructure their relationship dance. In therapy sessions, the therapist is a collaborator who must sometimes follow and sometimes lead, rather than an expert who instructs the couple on how their relationship should be. The therapy process presents the couple with opportunities to experiment with new ways to be together, so that they can make conscious choices about the kind of relationship they wish to create.

Focus on the Present

The EFT therapist focuses on the here-and-now responses of the partners, tracking and expanding both internal experiences and interactional moves and countermoves. Change occurs in the session as the couple experience themselves differently and interact in a new way. Attention is paid to family-of-origin issues only as they are played out in the here and now of the interaction, in contrast to object relations or analytic approaches to marital therapy or systemic Bowenian approaches, which focus more on the past, using techniques such as the construction of genograms. There is also less use of future-oriented interventions such as the assigning of future tasks

and homework, which are important interventions in the behavioral tradition.

Treatment Goals

The goal of EFT is to reprocess experience and reorganize interactions to create a secure bond between the partners—a
sense of secure connectedness. The focus here is always on
attachment concerns, on safety, trust, and contact, and on the
obstacles to all of these. There is, then, no attempt to teach a
distressed couple communication skills per se, since from the
EFT perspective it is unlikely that couples will use such skills
when they are most relevant, that is, when each becomes distressed and vulnerable. Since partners' problems are generally
not viewed as resulting from personality flaws, there is little
emphasis on insight into unconscious, intrapsychic conflicts.
Indeed, insight is considered insufficient for creating lasting
change in emotionally charged interactional patterns. Also,
since the relationship is primarily considered as a bond rather
than a rational bargain, there is no attempt to help the couple
renegotiate new deals or resolve pragmatic issues by drawing
up new agreements or contracts.

An Emotional Focus

Emotion is seen as the primary player in the drama of marital
distress and in changing that distress. It is emotion that organizes attachment behaviors, orients and motivates us to respond to others, and communicates our needs and longings to
them. In EFT, emotion, rather than being minimized, controlled, or simply labeled, is developed and differentiated.
Emotional experience and expression are viewed to a much
greater extent as targets and agents of change than they are in
other nonexperiential models of therapy. The expansion and
articulation of new aspects of emotional experience are primary therapeutic tasks here, and a new corrective emotional
experience of engagement with one's partner is the essence of
change in EFT.

Taking People as They Are

Distressed partners are not seen primarily as deficient, developmentally delayed, or unskilled. Other authors have also suggested that a general view of marital problems as necessarily reflecting some form of significant developmental delay is often inappropriate (Gurman, 1992). Partners' needs, desires, and primary emotional responses are seen here as generally healthy and adaptive. *It is how these needs and desires are enacted in a context of perceived danger that creates problems.* Also, it is how emotional responses, such as fear, are inhibited, disowned, and distorted that leads to dysfunction. The therapist's role is to validate partners' experiences and responses, rather than teaching them to be different.

To put it more succinctly, people are seen as being stuck in particular absorbing emotional states and in self-reinforcing interaction cycles, rather than as being generally deficient. Partners are stuck in certain ways of processing, organizing, and regulating emotional experience. They are also stuck in set ways of relating to each other. It is assumed that, given their experience, individuals have coherent and valid reasons for constricting emotional processing and interactions with their spouse. It is the therapist's task to grasp the "hidden rationality" (Wile, 1981) behind seemingly destructive or irrational responses.

WHERE DOES EFT COME FROM?

EFT is essentially a synthesis of experiential and systemic approaches to therapy. It is experiential in that it focuses on:

- How people actively process and construct their experience in interactions with their environment in the present.
- The power of the therapist's empathy and validation in creating the most positive context for exploration and the creation of new experience.

- The great capacity that human beings have for growth and the positive adaptiveness of emotional responses and needs.

EFT is systemic in that it focuses on:

- The power of context. Each partner's behavior is seen in the context of, and as a response to, the other's behavior. Each partner also is seen as in some sense creating the responses of the other, often without any awareness of how this occurs.
- There is a constant focus on the structure and process of interaction, that is, on how such interaction is organized. Degrees of closeness/distance and dominance/submission are monitored and made explicit.
- The rigid, negative interactional cycles distressed couples generate are seen as self-maintaining and as a primary factor in the deterioration of the relationship.
- There is a focus on circular rather than linear causality. This lends itself to a focus on pattern and sequence and on how elements in an interactional pattern reciprocally determine each other, as in, "I withdraw because you nag, and you nag because I withdraw."

EFT synthesizes experiential and systemic approaches, combining the intrapersonal and the interpersonal. The EFT therapist helps partners to reprocess their emotional experience and uses emotional expression to create a shift in their interactional positions. The EFT therapist also directs and choreographs new interactions, which evoke new emotional responses in the partners. As previously stated, new emotional experience impacts how the couple dance together, and the new dance impacts how each partner's emotional experience is organized.

HOW IS EFT STRUCTURED?

EFT is designed to be implemented in 8 to 20 sessions of marital therapy. A positive therapeutic alliance with both partners is considered to be a prerequisite of successful treatment. It is not designed to be used with violent couples or separating couples. It appears to be most successful with couples who wish to restructure their relationship in terms of a closer bond and who have become alienated by negative interaction cycles, often of a blame/withdraw nature. It can also be used in a variety of populations, apart from maritally distressed couples. For example, it is used in a hospital clinic in a large, urban center, where couples generally present with multiple problems, including the symptoms of posttraumatic stress disorder and clinical depression. In a shortened form, it has also been used with nonclinical couples, who are experiencing a lack of intimacy, and with couples where one partner has suffered a recent stressor, such as a life-threatening illness, that requires a change in the couple's relationship. An observer in an EFT session would see the therapist moving between helping partners to crystallize their emotional experience and setting interactional processes in motion with specific tasks (e.g., Can you tell him . . . ?)

The couples change process has been delineated in the following nine steps:

Step 1. Assessment. Creating an alliance and delineating conflict issues in the core struggle.

Step 2. Identifying the negative interactional cycle.

Step 3. Accessing the unacknowledged emotions underlying interactional positions.

Step 4. Reframing the problem in terms of underlying emotions and attachment needs.

Step 5. Promoting identification with disowned needs and aspects of self and integrating these into relationship interactions.

Step 6. Promoting acceptance of the partner's experience and new interaction patterns.

Step 7. Facilitating the expression of needs and wants and creating emotional engagement.

Step 8. Facilitating the emergence of new solutions to old relationship problems.

Step 9. Consolidating new positions and new cycles of attachment behaviors.

These steps and the interventions and processes associated with them are discussed in Chapters 4 through 8.

THE PROCESS OF CHANGE IN EFT

The following three shifts are discernible in the process of EFT:

- Cycle de-escalation
- Withdrawer engagement
- Blamer softening

The first shift, cycle de-escalation, is a first order change; the way interactions are organized remains the same, but the elements of the cycle are somewhat modified. For example, the more withdrawn partner in a couple begins to risk more engagement in the relationship while the more hostile partner becomes less reactive and angry. The couple may begin to initiate some close contact such as lovemaking, seem to find their engagement in therapy reassuring, and begin to be hopeful about their relationship. The other two shifts represent second-order changes, in that they constitute a change in the structure of the relationship.

The second shift, withdrawer engagement, occurs when the more withdrawn partner begins to become more active and engaged in the relationship. This shift involves a change in interactional position, in terms of control and accessibility for contact. The withdrawn partner asserts his or her needs and wants—rather than stonewalling or avoiding the spouse—and becomes more and more emotionally engaged with the other in the therapy sessions.

The third shift, blamer softening, occurs when the previously hostile and more active spouse risks expressing his or her own attachment needs and vulnerabilities, allowing for interactions that challenge the trust level in the relationship. In the interests of clarity, these shifts have been presented as separate and independent. In practice, they are of course interwoven and reciprocally determining. As a critical spouse becomes less angry, the less engaged partner risks more involvement; as this involvement increases, the critical spouse allows him/herself to disclose needs and desires more openly. This then makes it easier for the less engaged partner to be responsive. Once these change events have reorganized the couple's interactions, prototypical bonding events can take place. Here, spouses can be open with each other about their needs and fears and renew their sense of the bond between them. These three shifts are illustrated in the following section.

A Typical Change Process: Snapshots

A couple enter therapy with the female partner complaining of lack of intimacy and her partner's absence from the relationship. The male partner complains of his spouse's aggression and unreasonableness, from which he withdraws. He believes the solution is to make love more often. She believes the solution is for her spouse to talk to her more. The therapist creates an alliance, assesses their relationship (see Chapter 4), and describes their pattern of pursue/blame and withdraw/placate to them, portraying them as creators and victims of the cycle. The highlights of the change process, if caught in snapshots, might then be as follows:

Cycle De-escalation

1. Gail (*pursuing wife*): "I am so angry. I have been so let down here. I've never felt so lonely. I want to show him he can't do this to me."

2. Ben (*withdrawing husband*): "No matter what I do, I get the message it's disappointing. I don't speak the language, and I don't know how to learn. I know I run away. I hide. I don't know what else to do."

3. Gail: "I know I push him away with my harping, but I get so panicked. (*to him*) I can't find you."

4. Ben: "I guess I developed the art of hiding. I never really thought that you were looking for me."

These statements include an awareness of the cycle, an owning of the person's part in the cycle, and a move to articulating underlying feelings, rather than blaming and avoiding. At this point, partners typically make comments like, "I'm finding out who you are in these sessions."

Withdrawer Engagement

1. Ben: "I'm never going to be the life and soul of the party. I don't want the pressure of that. I need a little recognition, though, when I do take risks with you. If you're going to keep writing report cards, then I'm going to play truant. And I don't want sex all the time. I do want to be held sometimes—and I don't want to feel so timid about asking for it."

In this kind of statement, Ben moves from self-protective distance to active assertive engagement. He talks of his attachment needs and his sense of self in relation to his wife. He is more accessible and engaged.

Blamer Softening

1. Gail: "I'm not sure this is going to work. I'll start to count on you, and you'll turn your back. It's been so long since I really felt safe with you."

2. Gail: " I want you to tell me that I come first with you. I have to know that I'm important, that you need to be close like I need to be close to you. That I am precious to you. I need to know.

Here, this partner reveals her vulnerability and places herself in the other's hands. When he then is able to respond, a healing, bonding event takes place that begins a new cycle of closeness and affirmation.

The purpose of this chapter has been to give the reader a sense of EFT and to place it in the context of the marital therapy field. Let us now turn to the philosophy behind EFT, starting with the EFT perspective on intimate relationships and continuing with the philosophy of therapeutic change.

2

SELF AND SYSTEM IN ATTACHMENT CONTEXTS: THE EFT PHILOSOPHY

Every therapist who observes the problems that clients bring to therapy has to answer the following list of three basic questions:

1. What is happening here? What is the problem? What is the target of intervention?
2. What should be happening here? What is healthy functioning? What is the goal of treatment?
3. What must the couple do to change the problem and move towards a healthier relationship? How can the therapist foster this change?

The answers to these questions provide a framework for understanding the multidimensional phenomena he or she is observing and will determine the therapist's focus and treatment strategies.

A therapist needs a theory of healthy functioning, including a formulation of how problems occur and disrupt such functioning as well as a theory of therapeutic change. In marital

17

therapy, the client is the relationship. A marital therapist, therefore, also needs a theory of adult intimacy and an understanding of the nature of adult love. This theory of adult love is the first topic in this chapter.

THE EFT PERSPECTIVE ON ADULT LOVE

The EFT therapist views adult love as a bond, an emotional tie with an irreplaceable other who provides a *secure base* from which to confront the world and a *safe haven*—a source of comfort, care, and protection. Attachment theory, as outlined in the work of John Bowlby (1969, 1988), is considered by many to be the best current theoretical model for understanding adult relationships. It appears to be more relevant to close interdependent relationships than exchange theory, which views adult relationships in economic terms, as negotiated quid pro quo agreements, and more inclusive and generative than analytic perspectives, which view adult relationships as being determined by unconscious conflicts from the past.

What is a bond, in attachment theory terms? A bond consists of behavioral, cognitive, and emotional elements. It involves a set of attachment behaviors, a set of emotional responses and strategies to regulate such responses, and an inner representation of prototypical interactions, which constitute working models of self and other in this context. Particular emphasis is placed here on emotional responses since emotional expression is the primary signaling system among intimates, and emotions activate and organize attachment behaviors.

The basic tenets of attachment theory and their significance for marital therapy are summarized here:

- Seeking and maintaining contact with others is a primary motivating principle in human beings. Dependency is an innate part of being human, rather than a childhood trait that we grow out of as we mature.

- Such contact is an innate survival mechanism. The presence of an attachment figure provides comfort and security, while perceived inaccessibility of such a figure creates distress. Positive attachments create a *secure base* (Bowlby, 1988) from which individuals can operate and most adaptively respond to their environment. Positive attachments also create a *safe haven* and so provide a buffer against the effects of stress and an optimal context for the continuing development of the adult personality.

- The building blocks of secure bonds are emotional accessibility and responsiveness, whether the relationship is between child and parent or between two adult partners.

- When the security of a bond is threatened, attachment behaviors are activated. If these behaviors fail to evoke responsiveness from the attachment figure, a prototypical process of angry protest, clinging, despair, and finally, detachment occurs.

- Individual differences in attachment styles have been identified in children and adults. In adults, four styles have been identified: secure, anxious, avoidant fearful, and avoidant dismissing (Bartholomew & Horowitz, 1991). These styles constitute predispositions to organize perceptions and responses in particular ways in intimate relationships. They can be viewed as possible answers to the basic question, "Can I count on my attachment figure to be available and responsive when needed?" (Hazan & Shaver, 1994). A particular way of viewing both the self and the other in intimate relationships has been found to be characteristic of each style.

  In the secure style, the self is viewed as basically lovable and others are viewed as generally reliable and responsive. Expectations are therefore positive and foster the development of trust and closeness. In the anxious style there is uncertainty as to the lovableness of self and the legitimacy of attachment needs, which renders dependency on others perilous and uncertain. In the avoidant styles, there is a distrust of others and a corresponding desire to limit any dependency on them.

These attachment styles, which arise from partners' past experience, can influence crucial relationship behaviors. For example, partners with avoidant styles tend to refrain from seeking and giving support when they or their partners become anxious; that is when they or their partner most need comfort. The working models that form the basis for such styles can change, however, as the person is exposed to new relationship experiences. At any time in a relationship, the quality of attachment will be the result of partners' attachment predispositions and present interactions that mediate the effects of such dispositions. It is important to note that styles are not viewed simply as maps or sets of expectations for relationships. They also imply *ways of processing attachment information* (Bretherton, 1990), influencing whether or not partners can readily access, process, and coherently communicate attachment information.

This perspective makes sense of key research findings on the nature of marital distress. First, it clarifies the finding that sustaining emotional engagement, rather than other factors, such as the ability to resolve arguments, predicts long-term marital satisfaction. This finding is consistent with an attachment perspective, which emphasizes the need for emotional contact between intimates. Disengagement and distance negate the attachment bond and, therefore, are at least as corrosive as angry fights, and probably more so. Second, the pattern of critical attack and nonresponsive withdrawal has been found to be particularly corrosive to adult relationships (Gottman, 1991). The attachment perspective suggests that this is because this pattern precludes any kind of safe, secure contact and therefore exacerbates attachment fears and anxieties. A consistent lack of response, for example, negates attachment bonds.

For the marital therapist, this theory, this lens on adult relationships, suggests certain ways of seeing couples' interactions and certain therapeutic responses. It suggests that distressed couples are most often engaged in a process of seeking security and contact in the face of perceived danger and a threat to their relationship. Angry criticism is often most usefully viewed, then, as an attempt to modify the other partner's inaccessibility and as a *protest response to isolation and abandonment by the partner.*

Avoidant withdrawal may be seen as an attempt to contain the interaction and regulate fears of rejection, thus avoiding the confirmation of working models concerning the unlovable nature of the self. An outline of some of the major implications of attachment theory for the marital therapist follows:

- The goal of marital therapy is to address attachment concerns, reduce attachment insecurities, and foster the creation of a secure bond. The main issues are connection and disconnection, separateness and closeness. Ideally, prototypical bonding events will be enacted in the therapy sessions, as when one partner expresses fear or hurt and the other provides comfort or one asks for acceptance and the other gives it. Attachment theory tells us what partners' needs are and why trust in one's partner's responsiveness is so crucial.

- The focus of therapy is upon attachment insecurities, longings, and needs. Therapy focuses upon the deprivation, loss of trust and connection, isolation, and attachment fears of the partners, and the ways in which their interaction patterns maintain this distress.

- Attachment theory is an interactional theory, where self and system define and determine each other. Problematic behavior is seen as a response to past and/or present threats to secure attachment. Problematic ways of dealing with attachment needs have evolved as ways of keeping past and/or present caregivers minimally accessible and thus maintaining the relationship. The focus on context, on the effects of real interactions with caregivers, makes this theory easily compatible with systems theory, which views each partner's behavior as constrained and organized by the other's responses in a particular context. It lends itself to an *interactional perspective* in which partners construct their relationships according to the maps they already possess, but new relationship events can also refocus such maps. The marital therapist is most effective when he or she works on both the intrapsychic and interpersonal levels. *In EFT, this perspective has fostered the tendency to use new emotional experience to create new points of contact, and new points of contact to create new emotional experiences.*

- Attachment theory places more emphasis on affect and is more specific as to its role in human functioning than other theoretical perspectives on intimate relationships. Emotional expression organizes interactions and communicates inner states to others. *It is the music of the attachment dance.*

  Emotional experience orients us to others and motivates us to seek out and respond to our attachment figures. Secure attachments also help us to regulate negative affect and to process information effectively. A focus upon emotion is, therefore, a key aspect of working with attachment concerns and difficulties. Specifically, particular attention should be paid to sadness and loss, to anger and protest, to fear and insecurity, as well as to the shame that arises when individuals have working models of the self as unacceptable.

- Attachment theory focuses on restructuring working models of self and other. As well as helping couples process attachment emotions and enact new attachment behaviors, attachment theory suggests that therapy must pay attention to the core cognitions concerning self and other. *Implicit and explicit self-definitions and definitions of the other emerge in emotionally charged marital interactions and become available for modification and reassessment.* A further differentiation and integration of self is often an essential part of the marital therapy process.

• The attachment lens is a depathologizing one. Attachment needs and desires are seen as essentially healthy
and adaptive. Attachment theorists, like experiential theorists such as Rogers (1951), see human beings as
"strongly inclined towards self-healing" (Bowlby, 1988,
p. 152). Attachment theory also specifically depatholog-
izes dependency, as do some schools of feminist thought
(Jordan, Kaplan, Miller, Stiver, & Surrey, 1991). It is how
partners process and enact such needs in a context of
perceived danger that gives rise to self-reinforcing negative interactional cycles, which become problematic.
This frame allows the therapist to validate dependency
needs in both men and women and help partners give
these needs a positive voice in their relationships.

This is a very different orientation from the concern
with processes such as differentiation, fusion, and indi-
viduation that have helped to shape the marital therapy
field. Specifically, extreme expressions of dependency
needs can be viewed as the effects of deprivation and
insecurity, which arise from the social context and the
quality of attachment relationships, and can best be rem-
edied by addressing such deprivation, rather than being
focused on as developmental deficits.

Pragmatically, using this attachment lens to look at marital
relationships allows the therapist to see through the complex-
ity of distressed interaction patterns to the simpler basic human needs and emotions that we all share and to validate these
needs and emotions. This, at the very least, builds a powerful
therapeutic alliance with each partner and, at best, provides
a focus and direction for effective intervention. *It also provides
a powerful way of reframing each partner's responses in a
distressed relationship in a manner that fosters compassion
and contact, rather than mistrust and alienation.* Placing an
anxious partner's critical pursuit of the other in an attachment
context reframes this behavior as a fear of loss and a compelling desire for the other partner, and this reframing helps to
foster responsiveness in the other partner.

If we consider the list of questions posed at the beginning of this chapter, concerning the nature of problems, health, and change, in the light of attachment theory, the following answers emerge. In a distressed relationship, a perceived lack of accessibility and/or responsiveness creates insecurity in at least one of the partners. Usually, this insecurity is not being addressed directly but is being expressed by critical pursuing or avoidant withdrawn behaviors, which create an interaction pattern that actually exacerbates each partner's insecurity and precludes safe emotional engagement. Such engagement would allow the attachment issue to be addressed and possibly resolved.

Attachment threat can arise as a result of how one processes events in the context of one's attachment style, as a result of present interactions, and/or some combination of these elements. In very distressed relationships, style and present recurring interactions often reinforce each other in a negative spiral of hostility and distance. More graphically, negative experience and negative interaction mesh in such a way as to put a *spin* on the negative cycle, creating a force field that sweeps everything up into its vortex. On a more general level, *distress arises because one or both partners' attachment needs are not being met; there is no secure base. This results in compelling anxiety, which constricts both information processing and social interaction.* The goal of therapy is to foster the development of safe contact, accessibility, and responsiveness in both partners and to make them aware of their attachment needs. To attain this, the couple have to deal with the powerful emotional responses that organize their interactions and access and restructure elements of their inner working models, if these are problematic. They then can engage in new attachment behaviors.

THE EFT THEORY OF CHANGE

As noted in Chapter 1, EFT is a synthesis of experiential and systemic approaches to therapy. It views marital distress as being maintained by the manner in which people organize and process their emotional experience and by the patterns of interaction they engage in that take on a life of their own and become self-reinforcing. A distressed couple are in an absorbing state of compelling, automatic emotional responses and a reciprocal set of rigidly organized interactions, both of which constrict interaction and experience. This absorbing state (where everything leads into and reinforces distress and nothing leads out) renders accessibility and responsiveness almost impossible.

Research has shown that distressed couples are distinguishable by their rigidly structured interaction patterns and their intense negative affect. What do the two approaches to change, the experiential and the systemic therapies, tell us about how to help couples redefine their relationships? The experiential perspective focuses on how to help partners reprocess their experience, and the systemic perspective focuses on how to help partners modify their interaction patterns.

The Experiential Viewpoint

What are the main tenets of experiential approaches to therapy that are relevant to the practice of EFT?

- Human beings are constantly processing and constructing their experience and symbolizing that experience. The client, not the therapist, is the expert concerning his or her own experience. The therapist's role is to help the client expand awareness of that experience, integrate aspects that were excluded from awareness, and create new meaning frameworks.

- It is the acceptance and empathy of the therapist that fosters a reprocessing of experience and the construction of new meanings.

- Human beings are oriented toward growth and development and in general have healthy needs and desires. It is the constriction, disowning, and denial of these needs

and desires that create problems. This therapeutic approach is compatible with attachment theory in that dependency needs and desires would tend to be seen as
basically adaptive, while the disowning or distortion of
these desires would be seen as problematic. The focus
here is on growth through new experience and new ways
of processing that experience, rather than on the correction of deficits or deficiencies. The focus is also on helping people become more of who they are and respecting
their way of being, rather than on replacing specific behaviors and cognitions so that they may act differently.

- Emotion is given a prime place in this approach, as it is
  in attachment theory. Emotional schemes are constructed in relation to situations that frustrate or satisfy
  needs and goals, and these schemes guide people in the
  differentiation and classification of experience and in organizing anticipations and reactions (Greenberg, Rice, &
  Elliott, 1993). They also guide information processing
  and organized responses to others. These schemes help
  us predict, interpret, respond to, and control our experience. Emotions are not stored but are reconstructed by
  the appraisal of a situation that activates a scheme—an
  organized set of responses. In therapy, such schemes are
  activated and made available for exploration and development; they also may be modified by new experience.

- The therapist is a creator of safety, who fosters intense
  and new experience, and a process consultant, who
  helps the client contact, explore, symbolize, and integrate new experience. Change occurs in the session, in
  the present, as a result of the expanded processing of
  experience and the generation of new experience, that
  modifies emotional schemes.

A marital therapist who is using an experiential approach
would do the following:

- Focus on and reflect each partner's emotional experience.

- Validate and accept that experience, rather than trying to replace it.
- Attune to and empathically explore such experience, focusing on what is most alive and poignant, the not-yet-quite-formulated felt sense that emerges.
- Expand the client's experiencing by questions, usually process questions, such as what or how, and by conjectures.
- Direct the client to engage in a task that fosters a new kind of processing of experience, such as attending to new elements in a problematic reaction, (e.g., the stimulus or trigger, rather than the reaction itself), and broadening and deepening this awareness until new facets emerge that reorganize the experience as a whole.

These interventions were originally designed for use in individual therapy. When using these interventions in marital therapy, the partner is observing while the therapist is helping his/her spouse reprocess experience. However, the therapist here is not conducting individual therapy in the presence of the other. *Rather, the goal for the exploration of intrapsychic experience is to foster a new kind of contact with the partner.* This influences the kinds of experience that the therapist will choose to focus on and how the therapist will intervene.

In couples therapy, there has to be a balance between exploring each partner's intrapsychic experience, validating each partner's very different experience, and encouraging interaction between the partners. The therapist also has to be aware that partners are witnessing and reacting to the therapist's interventions with their spouses and has to be acutely sensitive to how that partner is hearing the therapist's comments. The therapist must be sure, for example, that in validating one spouse he or she does not discount the other's experience.

If we answer the questions posed at the beginning of the chapter, in the light of experiential theory, the following answers emerge. Problems arise or are maintained when partners organize or process their experience in a constricted manner, limiting awareness, and rendering behavior inflexible. The goal of therapy is to help clients to expand their manner of processing, to symbolize their experience in a way that enables them to connect with their needs and goals, and to respond to their environment in new ways. Awareness of emotion is central to healthy functioning in this perspective, since emotional responses orient the individual to his or her own needs and longings. They also motivate that individual to contact the environment and to strive to meet those needs. The process of change here involves a more intense engagement with one's own experience and the creation of new experience and new meanings.

Systems Theory

What are the main tenets of systems theory that are relevant to the practice of EFT?

First, since many different kinds of systems orientations exist, it is best to define how this term is used. Systems theory here refers to the systemic structural approach as exemplified by the work of Minuchin and Fishman (1981). Systems theory places the focus on present interactions and the power of those interactions to direct and constrict individual behavior.

- Systems theory encourages us to look at a particular context as a whole and how elements of that context interact, rather than at one or two elements in isolation. The focus is on how elements are organized into predictable patterns. Parts can be understood only in the context of the whole, so one partner's behavior can be understood only in the context of the other partner's behavior. Cycles of interaction are the focus here.

- The elements of a system stand in consistent relationship to each other; they interact in predictable, organized ways that generate stability and coherence. In order to create change, a systems therapist will focus on changing the ways in which the elements in a system relate to each other, the way the system is organized, rather than the elements themselves. A focus on the process of interaction and how it is organized arises naturally from this perspective.

- Causality is circular, so no one behavior simply causes another; rather, each is linked in a circular chain to other behaviors, as when one partner nags in response to the other's withdrawal and the other withdraws in response to the nagging. The focus is not on inner motives and intentions but on the pull of each partner's behavior on the other. This perspective encourages the therapist to discover how each partner inadvertently helps to create the other's negative responses in the circular feedback system of mutual influence.

- The emphasis is on the communicative aspects of behavior, the command or relationship-defining element inherent in how things are said, which then defines the role of the speaker and listener, rather than on content. This allows the therapist to focus on each partner's interactional position in terms of closeness and distance, autonomy and control. This is of crucial importance in understanding cycles and each person's behavior in the cycle. How participants are defined in communication with significant others also influences how they see themselves, so changing relationship structure also affects intrapsychic responses to the self.

- The therapist's task is to change the negative, rigid, interactional cycle the couple consistently engage in. This can be done in various ways: by reframing interactional positions to create new perceptions and responses or by interrupting interactional patterns with tasks, such as sharing fears, that create a new kind of dialogue. To be effective, the therapist has to join with the couple system and create an alliance.

- The goal of structural systemic interventions is to restructure interactions in such a way as to foster flexibility (which allows partners to adapt effectively to changing contexts) and the growth of individuals in the relationship. In other words, the goal is to create a system that supports belonging and autonomy and that fosters contact, while allowing for individual differences and desires. Where there is a secure bond, individual differences are not threatening but are in fact enlivening. As Minuchin and Nichols (1993) state, "to be more fully connected is to be more fully oneself" (p. 286).

How does systems theory answer the questions posed at the beginning of the chapter as to the nature of the problem, the goal of therapy, and the nature of change? The problem in systemic terms is the structure of the relationship, the positions the partners adopt, and the process of interaction—that is, the tight repetitive sequences of self-reinforcing responses typically found in distressed relationships. The goal is to foster more flexible positions and new kinds of interactions, thus allowing each partner to have a sense of control and belonging in the relationship.

Integrating Systemic and Experiential Perspectives

These two ways of creating change work well together—they make good partners. They are easily integrated and also complement each other, each bringing a different perspective, one intrapsychic and one interpersonal. Both view the person as a fluid system constantly in the process of creation, rather than as possessing a fixed character based on psychogenetic determinants. Both focus on the present rather than on historical determinants as important causes of specific behaviors. In both approaches, people tend to be seen as "stuck" rather than deficient or sick. In the experiential approach, people are caught in constricted ways of processing information and in emotional schemes that limit their responses. In systemic approaches, people are constrained by the interactional patterns or rules of the relationship. In both approaches, the therapist has to join or ally with the couple and help them create new more flexible positions, patterns, and ways of processing their inner worlds.

In the EFT perspective, it is necessary for the marital therapist to use a model of change that incorporates the intrapsychic and the interpersonal. The research on marital distress also suggests that it is necessary for marital therapy to address both the negative interaction patterns and the powerful negative emotional responses that distressed couples exhibit. It seems logical, then, that an integrated combination of experiential and systemic interventions would be effective in helping distressed couples redefine their relationship. The experiential model gives the therapist a guide to accessing and reprocessing emotional experience, and the systemic model gives the therapist a guide to restructuring interactions.

SUMMARY: THE PRIMARY ASSUMPTIONS OF EFT

Using attachment theory as the basis for understanding adult love and an experiential and systemic approach to therapeutic change, what then are the main assumptions of EFT?

- The most appropriate paradigm for adult intimacy is that of an emotional bond. The key issue in marital conflict is then the security of this bond. Such bonds are created by accessibility and responsiveness and, by emotional engagement. These bonds address our innate need for security, protection, and contact.
- Emotion is key in organizing attachment behaviors and in organizing the way the self and the other are experienced in an intimate relationship. Both attachment and experiential theory stress the importance of emotional experience and expression. Emotion guides and gives meaning to perception, motivates to action, and communicates to others. It is both a crucial target and an agent of change in marital therapy. The creation of new emotional experience is considered the most important factor in both intrapsychic and interpersonal change.

- Problems in relationships are maintained by the way interactions are organized and by the dominant emotional experience of each partner in the relationship. These elements operate in a reciprocally determining manner and can be used in therapy to mutually influence and redefine each other.

- The attachment needs and desires of partners are essentially healthy and adaptive. It is the way such needs and desires are enacted in a context of perceived insecurity that creates problems. Both attachment theory and the experiential view of human functioning emphasize the potentially adaptive nature of most needs and desires and see problems arising from the disowning and constriction of such needs. The recognition and validation of such needs is a key part of EFT.

- Change in EFT is associated with the accessing and reprocessing of the emotional experience underlying each partner's position in the relationship. The creation of new emotional experience and new ways of expressing that experience tends to modify the positions partners take with each other and allows for new interactions to occur, which then redefine the relationship. Change does not occur through insight, catharsis, or negotiation—it occurs through new emotional experience and new interactional events.

This chapter has outlined the theoretical perspectives that the EFT therapist uses to understand relationships and to guide his/her interventions. The next chapter outlines the basic therapist skills necessary for the successful implementation of EFT.

3

EXPANDING EXPERIENCE AND SHAPING DANCES: BASIC THERAPIST SKILLS IN EFT

Therapist: So that expression, when she lifts her eyebrows, touches off a sense of doom in you (*he nods*), a kind of sinking hoplesness (*he nods*), that she is never going to hear you, see you, let you close. There's no chance.

Husband: Yeah, so I clam up. I go numb. She'll never trust me.

Therapist: Yes, can you tell her about the sinking hopelessness, right now. Can you turn your chair and tell her how it feels?

The EFT therapist has to be able to create a safe context for both partners, a secure base in attachment theory terms, in order to access emotion and restructure interactions. This involves an ability to flexibly move from processing inner experience with an individual to choreographing interactions between partners, from following and tracking experience and interactions to moving such experience and interactions forward. The therapist needs to be able to hold experiential and systemic perspectives simultaneously; to see how a particular spouse's silent withdrawal is an almost inevitable response given the partner's behavior and, at the same time, to also see how this spouse's way of organizing his experience, his style,

plays a part in this withdrawal and tends to dictate his partner's behavior.

It is easier to learn EFT if the therapist's personal style includes, as well as the flexibility mentioned above, a certain
comfort with emotional experience and with being active and
directing interactions. The process of EFT involves fostering
intense experience and pointed, sometimes dramatic, encounters. It is an "up close" type of therapy, rather than a therapy
that advocates a detached therapeutic stance. The therapist
needs to have some level of comfort with relatively close contact. The EFT therapist is active, engaged, and flexible. The
person of the therapist is an important factor here, but there
are also set techniques and interventions that have proven effectiveness. The EFT therapist uses his/her personal style and
resources to create a context for techniques and interventions
and to connect with each client's experience. The three basic
tasks involved in the successful implementation of EFT are:

1. The creation and maintenance of a consistent positive
   therapeutic alliance with both partners.
2. The accessing and reprocessing of emotional experience.
3. The restructuring of interactions.

TASK 1: THE CREATION AND MAINTENANCE OF A THERAPEUTIC ALLIANCE

In EFT, the therapeutic alliance is characterized by the therapist's being able to be with each partner as that partner encounters his/her emotional responses and enacts his/her
position in the relationship. The therapist is a collaborative
partner in the processing of experience and a guide in the
creation of a new relationship dance. The therapist acts as a
process consultant, not as an expert on the contents of each
partner's psyche or on the right way to construct an intimate
relationship. A positive alliance is one in which the client sees

the therapist as appropriately warm and supportive, views the tasks presented by the therapist as relevant and helpful, and shares the same therapeutic goal as the therapist. The client then has confidence that the therapist will be accepting and able to help with the painful experiences and destructive cycles that are part of marital distress.

The building of this alliance is an inherent part of the interventions used in the beginning sessions of EFT, both in interventions that focus on individual experience and in interventions that focus on interactions. Both the reflection and validation of each partner's experience of, and position in, the relationship and the description of how interactional cycles are organized are powerful interventions in and of themselves; they also build a strong alliance. Both partners then experience the therapist as someone who can and does empathize with them and also understands the powerful web of interactions in which they are caught. These interventions are described in more detail in Chapters 4 and 5.

In more general terms, the most powerful element in the building of an alliance is the stance the therapist takes towards the couple, their distress, and change. In EFT, this stance is characterized by the following:

Empathic Attunement. There is a constant attempt by the therapist to empathically attune to each partner and to connect on a personal level. Empathy has been described as an act of imagination, an ability to inhabit each client's world for a moment (Guerney, 1994). In experiential approaches, the taking of this stance, together with its communication to the client, has traditionally been seen as curative in and of itself (Rogers, 1951). It reduces anxiety and allows for a more complete engagement in ongoing experience. The therapist is concerned not with evaluating the client's comments in terms of truth, realism, or psychopathology, but rather in making contact with the client's world. The focus is, what is it like to be this client in this context? Therapists' ability to listen, to connect what they hear with their own experience, and then stay with this subjective perspective enables them to answer this question.

Acceptance. A nonjudgmental stance is essential in the creation of a powerful alliance. This stance is somewhat a function of who the therapist is and how aware this person is of his/her own human frailties and vagaries, but it is also a function of the theories and beliefs he/she holds. It is difficult to hold and communicate a nonjudgmental stance if the therapist adheres to a model of therapy that can view people as deficient or defective. It is easier to maintain such a stance if the therapist has a relatively positive view of human nature and a belief in people's ability to change and grow. The experiential approach to therapy has emphasized the need for the therapist to honor and prize clients as they are and to be able to tolerate aspects of clients that even they do not prize or accept. This stance of respect and acceptance allows partners to face, with the therapist, what they could not face alone or reveal to the other partner.

Genuineness. The genuineness of the therapist, how real and present he/she is able to be, is a crucial aspect of the alliance. This does not mean that the therapist is impulsive or self-disclosing, but rather that the therapist is accessible and responsive to the client in a way that the client can trust. The therapist can then admit mistakes and *allow clients to teach him/her about their experience.* In short, the therapeutic relationship is a real human encounter, which the therapist takes on with integrity, although the alliance with marital partners may not have the intensity of the alliance in individual therapy. This intensity is mediated in marital therapy by the presence of probably the most important attachment figure in each individual's life, the other partner.

Active Monitoring. If this kind of alliance is to be maintained throughout therapy, the therapist must take an active deliberate role in monitoring, probing, and, if necessary, restoring this alliance. The therapist monitors his/her engagement with each spouse, actively seeking and processing each partner's responses to him/her. If the therapist has any hint that there may be a rupture in the alliance, the mending of this alliance becomes an immediate priority. The therapist might ask questions as to a client's reactions to his/her comments or interventions, encouraging the expression of the client's own views and desires. An empathic question from the therapist can strengthen the alliance and/or prevent a rupture in it. For example, at the end of a session, a therapist might state that the couple had worked pretty intensely and invite their reactions, particularly concerns about the process or content of the session. The therapist then explicitly encourages the partners to give feedback to him/her.

Joining the System. The marital therapist engages not only each spouse, but also the relationship system. The therapist sees and accepts the relationship as it is structured at the beginning of therapy. In systemic terms, the therapist joins the system. This involves the therapist not only capturing and being able to describe the specific positions and patterns in the relationship, but being able to accurately reflect to the couple their own idiosyncratic version of the general cycles distressed couples evolve together. The most common of these cycles is attack/pursue defend/withdraw. The therapist reflects the sequence and pattern of interactions, in an empathic, and respectful manner, allowing the couple to take a metaperspective on their interactions. They can then own a part in the creation of the pattern, while also being acknowledged as its victims.

The therapist has to be able to validate each partner's experience of, and position in, the relationship in the presence of the other without in any way invalidating the other's experience. Each partner also sees the therapist and the other spouse relating to each other and this may be a crucial part of the alliance and of the general change process. The spouse, for example, may reveal him/herself in a new way in the interaction with the therapist. For the therapist, this demands a high level of awareness as to how interventions with one spouse may affect the other, and a willingness to focus on this. For example, the therapist may ask for a partner's reaction to the dialogue he/she has just had with the other spouse and find out that the partner sees the other as receiving preferential treatment from the therapist, or that witnessing the dialogue evoked resentment as to why a spouse could reveal to the therapist what he/she could not reveal to the partner.

The stance just described elicits a collaborative partnership between the couple and the therapist, which is explicitly delineated in the early sessions by an exploration of the goals of therapy and the kinds of tasks that the therapist will be asking the couple to engage in. Part of the assessment process in EFT is clarifying each partner's goals and ascertaining whether these are compatible, as well as clarifying what partners can expect from therapy .

TASK 2: THE ACCESSING OF EMOTION

Emotional experience is focused upon, expanded, reprocessed, and restructured throughout the process of EFT. The expression of new and/or expanded emotional experience then allows for a reorganization of the interactional positions partners take with one another. The accessing of desperate loneliness in a critical attacking partner, for example, a) creates a new meaning context for this partner's hostility, b) allows this hostility to be reprocessed as desperation, fostering a new presentation of self to the other, and c) challenges the other's perceptions of this hostile partner's behavior and thus fosters new responses towards this partner. The accessing of emotion is particularly important at particular times in therapy, specifically in Steps 3 and 5, as described later in Chapters 5 and 6.

Emotion in EFT

Before describing the basic skills involved in this task, it is important to clarify how emotion is conceptualized in EFT. It is also important to note, since emotion is a global label applied to many different experiences from embarrassment to despair, that this term refers here to the small number of basic universal emotions identified by theorists (Izard, 1977; Plutchik, 1980). More specifically, in this volume, it refers to anger, fear, surprise, hurt/distress, shame, sadness/despair, and joy.

Emotion is seen here in information processing terms, as an integration of physiological responses, meaning schemes, and action tendencies, as well as the self-reflexive awareness of this experience. Emotion is a rich source of meaning, it gives us powerful compelling feedback as to how our environment is affecting us. This feedback regulates our responses, and organizes our behavior. Emotional expression, by communicating with others, also regulates social interaction. Emotions orient us to our world and provide us with crucial information about the personal significance of events; they tell us what we want and need.

Emotion is seen here as basically adaptive, providing a response system that is able to rapidly reorganize a person's behavior in the interests of security, survival, or the fulfillment of needs. In intimate relationships, affect tends to:

- *Focus attention and orient partners to their own needs and particular environment cues.* So when I am sad, I am acutely aware of how much I need contact, and I am particularly sensitive to any sign of distancing by my partner.

- *Color perceptions and meaning construction.* So my anger primes me to see the other's behavior as an affront to me and reminds me of all the other incidents that I experienced in the same way.

- *Prime and organize responses, particularly attachment behaviors.* When I am anxious, I am particularly likely to seek out my partner for reassurance and comfort.

- *Activate core cognitions concerning, self, other, and the nature of relationships.* When I am engaged in an emotionally hot interaction, key defining concepts about myself naturally arise, such as, "Perhaps I deserve this response. I am inadequate."

- *Communicate with others.* Emotion is the primary signaling system in analogic, relationship-defining interactions. It pulls for particular responses from others and
  thus plays a crucial role in organizing interactions. When
  vulnerability is expressed, it tends to disarm and pull
  for compassion, while anger tends to pull for compliance
  and/or distance. Intense emotion also tends to override
  other cues and elicit compelling responses, such as fight/
  flight or approach/avoid. These responses are difficult
  to inhibit or control and then tend to constrain the responses of the other partner. Emotion is the music in the
  dance of adult intimacy.

Emotion is compelling and powerful, particularly in intimate relationships. If it is not enlisted into the service of therapy, it is at the very least a powerful force left unused, and at
worst it can be an active undermining agent. A focus on emotion is also efficient, in that strong affective responses are able
to reorganize responses quickly and create broad changes of
perspective or meaning frameworks. As Sartre suggests, emotion involves a transformation of the world; to a sad man, it
is always raining. It can be used to transform the world into
a more positive place, full of new possibilities.

Emotion is supremely relevant here. In distressed attachment relationships, where responses have high emotional impact, a corrective experience has to evoke emotion. It is the
difference that makes a difference. It has been suggested that
"While thinking usually changes thoughts, only feeling can
change emotion" (Guidano, 1991, p. 61). It is interesting to
note here that when partners are trying to cope with and reorganize threatening emotions, they often do so by evoking a
competing alternative emotion. Fear, for example, often elicits
an angry response.

Emotion can be differentiated into primary, secondary, instrumental, and maladaptive responses (Greenberg & Safran,
1987). Primary emotions are here-and-now direct responses to
situations; secondary emotions are reactions to, and attempts

to cope with, these direct responses, often obscuring awareness of the primary response. For example, angry defen-
siveness is often expressed in marital conflict, rather than hurt,
fear, or some other primary affect. Instrumental emotions are
used to manipulate the responses of others. Maladaptive responses are out-of-context compelling responses that constrict
how present situations are processed, for example, the present
relational experience of abuse survivors is often colored by
the panic and numbing associated with the original abuse. *It
is the primary emotional responses that are unattended to,
undifferentiated, or disowned that the EFT therapist focuses
upon, although therapy often begins with the therapist reflecting and validating the secondary responses that the couple habitually present as part of the cycle of distress.*

Maladaptive responses are also part of the change process
in that, when they are acknowledged and expressed, their referent in past experience and how they are evoked in the present can be clarified. The present relationship can then become
a place where such emotions can be regulated in a different
manner and eventually restructured. For example, when a previously abused partner can acknowledge to self and other the
panic that arises during close physical contact, this often
evokes compassion and comforting behavior from the other
spouse, allowing new healing emotional experiences to occur
in the present relationship.

It is, then, the experience and expression of the primary
emotions underlying interactional positions, the sense of loss
underlying critical anger, or the helplessness and sense of failure underlying withdrawal that have the potential to create
new levels of emotional engagement and to modify interactional cycles in couples therapy. The differentiation of the
kinds of emotion outlined above is not difficult to make in
clinical contexts and emerges naturally out of the process of
therapy.

It is also important to clarify issues concerning the level
of emotion and how it is used in EFT. These issues can be
outlined as:

- *Involvement.* Emotional experience is not discussed from a distance with limited involvement. It is evoked and experienced as vividly and intensely as possible. It is this engagement with emotional responses that allows for the discovery of new aspects of each partner's emotional life and the reorganization of emotional schemes and experience. The therapist tends to use simple, concrete words and images that connect the person to that experience, rather than abstract terms or interpretations.

- *Exploration.* The goal here is *not* to place labels on experience or to teach clients better ways to express themselves. Rather, a process of emotional exploration and discovery is engaged upon, which expands each partner's experience of self in relation to the other. This involves focusing on the as yet unclear edges of experience and the differentiation and symbolizing of that experience. For example, this may involve unpacking a label like anger into different elements, such as exasperation, bitterness, helplessness, and fear. It may also involve focusing on background elements, such as the sensation of falling in the pit of the stomach, which is experienced very fleetingly just before a person becomes numb and distances from the spouse.

  When such elements are explored, new facets emerge that expand the experience as a whole and can be used to reorganize it. For example, numbness, when more fully processed, may become hopelessness and defiance. The experience and expression of these emotions then allows the partner's experience of self to evolve beyond numbness. To articulate that one is numb is often the first step away from numbness and towards connection with the partner. It also places this person's distance in a new meaning context for the partner and so creates a new kind of dialogue.

- *New Emotion.* The indiscriminate ventilation of negative emotion to create catharsis is *not* part of the EFT process and can be detrimental in couples therapy. The repetitive expression of secondary reactive emotions is an essential part of distressed couples' everyday problematic interactions. It is the discovery and development of new or unrecognized emotional experience that is useful in couples therapy.

Which Emotion to Focus on?

In terms of which emotion to focus on, the EFT therapist has three general guides.

- The therapist focuses upon the most poignant and vivid aspect of experience that arises in the therapy process, for example, the tear, the dramatic nonverbal gesture, the potent image or label.
- The therapist focuses upon the emotion that is salient in terms of attachment needs and fears.
- The therapist focuses on the emotion that seems to play a role in organizing negative interactions and restricting accessibility and responsiveness. The therapist focuses, then, upon the brief look of fear that occurs just before a withdrawn partner's statement of resignation and lapse into distant silence.

The therapy process also dictates which emotion the therapist will pick up and work with. In the beginning of therapy, for example, the therapist will be reflecting and validating secondary emotions such as anger, whereas in the middle phase of therapy the therapist will focus more on the underlying emotion, such as the helplessness that fuels the angry response. These underlying emotions are often implicit but not yet clearly formulated and/or articulated. They have an emerging or "leading edge" (Wile, 1994) quality to them.

The client's response also dictates the intensity of the therapist's focus. *The EFT therapist stays close to the client's experience, to where the client is in the here and now.* The readiness of the client to stay with and inhabit an emotion is also a factor here. A particular partner may be willing at a particular point in time to include confusion or discomfort in his/her construction of experience but may not be ready to formulate certain elements of his/her experience as fear.

SKILLS AND INTERVENTIONS: ACCESSING EMOTION

Reflection

The therapist attends to, focuses on, and reflects present poignant emotion. The therapist conveys understanding of the client's experience and directs the client's attention to that experience. Reflection here is not simply echoing and paraphrasing the client's words. It requires intense concentration from the therapist and an empathic absorption in the client's experience. The therapist tracks the client's experience, processing that experience with the client and being aware of how this particular client constructs his/her experience moment to moment.

If such reflection is skillfully done, the client feels seen and acknowledged. The therapy session then becomes a safe place and the therapist is seen as an ally. Such reflection also directs the clients' attention to their inner experience and slows down the interpersonal process in the session, underscoring the significance of particular comments and creating a focus for the process of therapy.

EXAMPLE

Therapist: So, help me understand, Ellen, what you are saying to Peter is, "I don't see that you want me and miss me. What I see and hear is that I am never enough. I disappoint you. I am analyzed and found wanting. I feel put down and defeated." Is that it?

Wife: Yes, that's it. I am condemned.

Validation

The EFT therapist conveys to both partners that they are entitled to their experience and emotional responses. If necessary, the therapist explicitly differentiates one partner's experience from the other's intention and/or character. So a partner can legitimately feel hated, without the other being hateful. The therapist takes the stance that there is nothing wrong, irrational, deficient, shameful, or strange about their responses. Empathic reflection, if it is done with respect and caring, conveys this message, but it is also necessary to explicitly validate each partner's experience of the relationship. The therapist's affirmation and the security created by this acceptance act as an antidote to the general level of anxiety and the climate of disqualification and self-protectiveness that characterizes distressed couples. This acceptance also acts as an antidote to the constricted experiencing and presentation of self, which result from self-criticism or from the anticipated judgment of others. Empathic reflection and validation encourage partners to become more engaged with their experience, so that this experience can be expanded upon and crystallized.

EXAMPLE

Therapist: I think I understand. It's like when he would say how depressed he was, you would feel overwhelmed and a little scared. You felt like this heavy weight was descending on you, crushing the breath out of you. So, after a while it was natural to push back at the weight, so you could breathe, and to get angry at your husband for not finding a way out. So you would withdraw or tell him to snap out of it. Is that it ?

Evocative Responding: Reflections and Questions

These responses focus upon the tentative, unclear, or emerging aspects of a partner's experience. The therapist attempts to vividly capture the quality and the implicit elements of this experience, tentatively expanding such experience, often by the use of evocative imagery. This then helps the client to construct this experience in a more differentiated way.

These reflections are offered *tentatively,* for the client to taste, try on, correct, reshape, or take on, not as an expert synopsis of his/her responses. The reflections may focus upon how cues are perceived and processed, the most poignant elements of an emotional or body response, the desires and longings that arise from a particular response, the conflicting elements within that response, or the action tendency or intention that is inherent in the emotional experience. The therapist guides clients to the *leading edge of their experience* and invites them to take another step in formulating and symbolizing the experience.

EXAMPLES

Therapist: So what is it about Mary's tone of voice right now that seems to trigger the sense of the floor dropping away?

Therapist: When you say that, Sam, there is a catch in your voice, like it hurts you to even put it into words, that you may not be what Mary needs.

Therapist: I'm unclear here, I think I hear you saying that when you see that expression on her face, you have this incredible desire to run and hide. Is that it? Help me understand.

Therapist: You want to run and hide, but some other part of you insists that you try to stand your ground, is that it?

Therapist: So when you hear that, part of you, the defiant part, wants to yell, "I'm never going to let you hurt me like that again." Is that it?

Questions such as: What happens to you when . . . How do you feel as you listen to . . . or as you say . . . What is it like for you . . . directly ask the client to differentiate his/her experience. The focus here may be on inner experience or on the process of interaction.

Therapist: What happens to you when you begin to feel this sense of hopelessness you just mentioned?

Therapist: What just happened there? Mary, you flinched when Jim hit his leg with his hand, and then you remained silent. What happened for you right then?

As part of capturing a client's experience the therapist may direct attention to a specific element. This may be done by simply repeating a poignant phrase that the client glossed over or did not emphasize, or by asking the client to repeat it.

Therapist: Can you say that again Mary, that piece where you said, I'm not going to let you destroy me.

These interventions are invitations to partners to explore and reprocess their experience. As they become more and more engaged with and immersed in their experience, new elements begin to arise that reshape that experience.

These interventions may vary in focus from helping clients contact their general experience of self and other in the relationship to helping clients reprocess a particularly loaded response that underlies their interactional position, to developing and restructuring specific compelling emotional responses in a way that helps to create accessibility and responsiveness in self and other.

Heightening

As the therapist tracks the internal and interpersonal processes, within each partner and between the couple, he/she may choose to highlight and intensify particular responses and interactions. These responses and interactions are often those that seem to play a crucial role in maintaining the couple's destructive interactions, although if positive or new interactions occur, these too are heightened. The therapist can use this heightened emotion to help partners engage with their emotional experience in a new way and create a different kind of dialogue with the other. Heightening brings a particular response from the background into the limelight, so that it can be used to reorganize experience and interaction. There are several ways of achieving this:

1. Repeating a phrase to heighten its impact.
2. Intensifying the experience by how something is said. The EFT therapist typically leans forward and lowers and slows his/her voice when heightening a response.
3. Using clear poignant images and metaphors that crystallize experience.
4. Directing partners to enact their responses; so as to turn intrapsychic experience into direct interpersonal messages.
5. Maintaining a specific focus. The therapist blocks exits or changes in the flow of experience that are likely to lessen the emotional intensity of the moment.

EXAMPLE

An excerpt of therapy illustrating the above interventions follows:

Therapist: So can you say that again Jim, I just can't open up and let myself commit to her.

Jim: Yes, I just can't. I can't make myself. I hold back. Keep her out.

Therapist: How do you feel as you say this, Jim?

Jim: I feel sad, but it feels right, it's right. It feels better.

Therapist: It feels safer to keep her on the other side of the door, to keep her at a distance.

Jim: Yes, it's just the way it is. In my country . . . .

Therapist: You want to keep her out. It feels better behind the door.

Jim: Yes.

Therapist: So can you tell her: I'm going to keep you out, at a certain distance. It really doesn't matter what you do. I'm not ready to put myself in anyone's hands. I'm not going to let you really connect with me.

The client begins to give his version of the therapist's statement and bursts into tears. In this moment, Jim's experience is intensified and his interactional position is enacted explicitly.

Empathic Conjecture/Interpretation

Here the EFT therapist infers the client's current state and experience from nonverbal, interactional, and contextual cues to help the client take his/her experiencing one step further. The aim here is not to comment on psychogenetic causes or patterns, or to help the client interpret his/her experience differently, but to extend and clarify that experience, so that new meaning can naturally emerge. Such conjectures are not cognitive labels that categorize and therefore provide closure to experience, and are not meant to give clients new information about themselves. The goal is to facilitate more intense experiencing, from which new meanings spontaneously arise, not to create insight per se. The inferences used here arise from the therapist's empathic immersion in the client's experience and his/her knowledge of the interactional positions and patterns of the couple. Such inferences are also guided by attachment theory, the perspective on adult love that forms the basis of EFT.

There is a concern, from an experiential perspective, that these interpretations not be in any way imposed upon the client by the therapist and so impede the client's discovery of his/her own awareness. This danger is reduced in couples therapy since the system and problematic responses are all visible to the therapist, and therefore immediate corrective feedback is available to challenge incorrect inferences. The inferences are also given in a tentative manner, and partners are actively and explicitly encouraged to guide and correct the therapist throughout therapy.

Inferences in EFT might typically concern defensive strategies and core catastrophic attachment fears and fantasies. These conjectures may take the form of statements concerning the need for self-protection apparently experienced by the partners, and formulations of attachment responses such as grief, the longing for comfort, or fears such as engulfment, rejection, and abandonment. The definitions of self implicit in partners' dialogue, such as the perceived unworthy or unlovable nature of the self, are also made explicit in this manner. The therapist thus elaborates on the partners' experience, or makes explicit the elements in that experience that they seem unable to formulate, or cannot yet own.

EXAMPLES

1. **Therapist:** So, the sense I get, Sam, is that you're caught between telling Marie to go to hell, no one is going to crowd you with expectations and demands, and no one is going to take you over and desperately fearing her anger and rejection, her dismissal of you. Is that right?

    Sam: Yeah, that sums it up; that's it exactly

2. **Therapist:** Where are you right now, Carrie?

    Carrie: Don't know.

    Therapist: What is happening?

    Carrie: Don't know . . . just feel quiet.

    Therapist: It's like you're a long long way away.

    Carrie: Yes, far away.

    Therapist: Where no one can hurt you, yes? (*Carrie nods vigorously.*) It's the only way to feel safe right now, is that it?

    Carrie: Right, I space right out.

    Therapist: What's it feel like, being spaced out?

    Carrie: Empty, but it's better than, than (*long pause*) . . .

Therapist: Than being humiliated and shamed, is that it?

Carrie: Yes, I asked him, and he laughed at me, just now, he laughed.

Therapist: Like you didn't matter, your longing didn't matter, like you were nothing, yes?

Carrie: I won't plead and beg, he'll wait a long time for that. I won't fight for him to listen.

Therapist: You'll go where he can't find you, and so defeat him, right? (*Carrie nods.*) It's empty and lonely, but you're intact then?

The EFT therapist also occasionally uses a particular and more elaborate form of conjecture called a disquisition, when partners are particularly resistant to exploring their experience and the above techniques are proving to be ineffective. A disquisition is a story constructed and presented by the therapist about couples in general, or about types of marital problems. This story is presented as perhaps having some similarity to, or relevance for, the couple in therapy. It is designed to be an elaborate description of the patterns and responses of the couple in therapy, with conjectured underlying emotions woven into the story. The narrative is set up to reflect the therapist's understanding of the present couple's intrapersonal and interpersonal realities, in a discursive, nonthreatening manner. It is usually an expanded version of the story the couple have presented in therapy, but one that is more elaborated in terms of emotional experience and the links between that experience and how the couple respond to each other. The usual effect of this intervention is that one or both partners will identify with some aspect of the story and begin to relate it to their own experience. This is an indirect and very nonthreatening way of probing for certain experiences with a relatively closed partner or couple.

EXAMPLES

The therapist can use disquisitions to elaborate on a partner's experience in the destructive cycle:

Therapist: There's something here that reminds me of some of the other couples I have worked with, and this may be completely different for you, of course, it may not even be similar, but in some couples the more active partners get to the point where they want the other person to hurt too. To see that they can have an impact, an effect on this seemingly impervious contained person, and they end up just hammering away, just to show the other partner that they won't just be ignored and discounted. The other partner experiences this as an attack, relentless and overwhelming, and just digs deeper and deeper into a trench, burrows down, builds up his/her defenses. It's like a kind of, "You can't get me," but it gets a bit tiring, always listening for distant guns and getting ready to duck, always having to be ready to run or to hide. This all ends up being pretty awful for both of them. I'm not sure if you can relate to this at all?

The therapist can also use disquisitions to conjecture about experience that the client does not own. For example, a disquisition might be made in response to intrusive jealous behavior on the part of a very uncommunicative husband who listened in on his wife's phone calls to friends and is unable to discuss this behavior in the session.

Therapist: (*to the wife*) Well, I hear that you really find it hard to understand this behavior of Ted's, and he seems to have a hard time talking about it. I'm not sure what it's all about. I see that it makes you angry. The only chord it strikes for me is that it reminds me of a client I had who couldn't stand to go to parties with his wife. He slowly realized that when he heard her talk to her friends with a lilt in her voice, he felt incredible anguish and longing, because it reminded him that she used to talk to him that way once, and he used to feel special and loved. It reminded him that it wasn't that way anymore, that he had lost that, somehow; she didn't talk to him like that anymore. He felt excluded and sad, so he'd get very angry and ask her lots of questions about her conversations, and she would end up feeling intruded upon. But that was this other client. It may not be relevant or similar to you at all.

This intervention is aimed primarily at accessing the husband's experience, but is directed to the wife in the form of a story about someone else.

Self-Disclosure

This is not a large part of the EFT therapist's repertoire, particularly when EFT is compared to other humanistic experiential approaches (Kempler, 1981). It is generally limited and used for a specific purpose, such as to build an alliance and intensify validation of clients' responses, or as a form of joining with clients to help them identify elements of their own experience.

EXAMPLES

1. **Husband:** I feel so foolish, I guess I feel that I shouldn't let my anxieties get out of hand to the point where I can't even hear my wife.

   Therapist: Hm, well I know I find it hard to really take in anything when I'm scared. Being scared tends to take up so much space.

2. **Husband:** I think I can deal with anything. I don't feel much right now at all.

   Therapist: You see yourself as pretty resilient. (*He nods.*) Well, I'd like to just share that for me when I see the struggle you two are engaged in, with your wife reaching out and you staying behind your wall, I get sad. Right now it seems sad to me.

These interventions normalize and validate clients' responses, or attempt to evoke a more emotional response from a partner who seems cut off from his/her feelings.

Summary

The therapist's interventions presented above are based upon first accepting both partners as they are, and by this acceptance creating a context for the exploration and elaboration of experience. Particular responses and positions are generally developed and elaborated, rather than confronted or replaced by more "skillful" approaches. The EFT therapist will validate and help the partners explore potentially negative responses such as anger or silent withdrawal, rather than suggest or teach different responses.

Helping clients access, reprocess, and if necessary, reorganize their experience of self and other in an intimate relationship is a process of discovery and creation. The client discovers new elements of his/her experience that have been previously denied, brushed aside, or simply not formulated.

TASK 3: RESTRUCTURING INTERACTIONS

The two tasks, accessing/reprocessing emotions and restructuring interactions, are separated here for the sake of clarity, but in practice they are always intertwined. The EFT therapist is always using new emotional experience to create new kinds of dialogue and interactional events, which then impact the inner emotional life of the partners. Thus, the expression of newly experienced vulnerability creates a dialogue about a husband's longing for comfort from his wife, which elicits new responses from that spouse. In turn, the new dialogue, in which the husband risks being needy and then receives caring, expands his sense of longing and creates in him the first glimmers of trust. Self and system, dancer and dance, reflect and create each other.

In Task Three, the therapist does the following:

- Tracks and Reflects the patterns and cycles of interaction.
- Reframes problems in terms of context, that is, in terms of cycles.
- Restructures interactions by choreographing new events, that modify each partner's interactional position.

Tracking and Reflecting

The therapist tracks and reflects the process of interactions, in a manner similar to the way in which the therapist tracks and reflects the process of inner experience as each partner constructs that experience. The therapist, by describing the process and structure of interactions, focuses in on and clarifies the nature of the relationship between partners. Early in the therapy process, the therapist pieces together, from the couple's descriptions and from direct observation, the typical problematic interactions the couple engage in. This sequence of interactions is reflected back to the couple and identified in terms of a recurring pattern, the most common being some form of blame/defend or pursue/withdraw. As stated previously, the partners are framed as both the unwitting creators and victims of these negative interactional cycles.

The identification and continuing elaboration of the negative cycle of interaction throughout therapy externalizes the problem in a manner not unlike the narrative approaches to therapy (White & Epston, 1990). This provides an antidote to versions of the relationship problem that involve defects within either of the partners, and tends to defuse blaming and destructive arguments aimed at assigning responsibility for relationship distress. This formulation allows the partners to take some responsibility for the way the relationship has evolved, while framing the destructive cycle, rather than the other partner or their own failings, as the enemy. This destructive pattern of interactions is framed as having a life of its own and as defeating the couple's attempts at contact and caring. The partners can then begin to move toward each other, facing together the enemy that is robbing them of their relationship. The experience of a common external enemy creates a pull toward cohesion in the couple.

The description of interactional patterns, like the descriptions of inner experience, continues throughout therapy and becomes more elaborated and differentiated as time goes on. The EFT therapist focuses upon prototypical moments in the interaction when such negative patterns are operating and either accesses underlying emotions to expand the interaction or reflects and/or replays the interaction to crystallize the dance between the couple. The therapist may ask questions such as:

- What just happened there ? You said . . . , and then you said . . . .
- How do you react, want to respond, when he talks about this in this way?

The therapist then replays, describes, and summarizes the interaction in order to clarify and heighten interactional sequences and the positions the partners take with each other in terms of closeness/contact and power and control.

EXAMPLES

The following is a reflection of a destructive cycle in session one:

Therapist: So, let's see if I understand. What usually happens here is that you want more closeness with Walt and you try to talk to him about your feelings and the relationship, and Walt, you prefer to be doing activities or to be with lots of friends, so you find it hard to make the time for this. You are not sure you even know what Jane means by talking. And this has got to the point where, Jane, you see Walt as a roommate rather than a partner, and so you get pretty angry and critical of him, and Walt you try to avoid her anger, so you go out even more and are spending less and less time with Jane. Is that it?

The following is a reflection of the same cycle later in therapy:

Therapist: This is one of those times, Jane, is it, where you start to feel all alone, like Walt is indifferent to you? You feel invisible, and that stirs up indignation in you (*invisible and indignation are Jane's words from a previous session*), and you protest. You get mad and you "get in his face," as you put it.

Jane: Yes, and then he does his "I'm out of here" thing.

Therapist: Ah-ha.

Walt: There's no point in staying.

Therapist: The way you experience it, there's nothing you can do then. It seems hopeless.

Walt: Right, right, so I run. I go and find my friends.

Therapist: You run to a safer place, where nobody gets mad at you, or tells you they are disappointed in you. That's very difficult for you to hear?

In the following, the therapist replays a specific instance or enactment of the cycle and further differentiates a partner's position.

Therapist: Mary, what happened just then, you bit your lip, went silent, and turned to look out of the window. And Peter, you said, "You never listen, maybe I should find someone who will," and Mary, you replied, "That's right, maybe that's right." It sounds like what you are saying to Peter is, "I won't listen. I won't be critiqued any more. I'll become quiet and distant and shut you out." (*Position is made explicit and active.*) Peter, you sounded pretty angry and accusing. You were letting Mary know that you could leave, which is a pretty big threat, heh? Is that what it is like for you, Mary, it's like you're saying, "I'll shut you out?"

Mary: Yes, that's the place I get to. I won't be constantly criticized, analyzed, destroyed, I won't, so I go watch TV and all the other things he says I do. I shut him out.

Therapist: It's like you're protecting yourself; if you don't, you'll be destroyed.

Mary: If I listened to him, I'd feel like nothing, like no one. I'm never enough. Why does he want to be close to me if I'm so awful.

Therapist: If you let him close, the message you expect to hear is that you are awful, nothing, almost unlovable. (*Mary agrees.*) So you shut him out. (*Mary nods her head.*)

Reframing

As a result of the tracking, identification and elaboration of the cycles of interaction referred to above, the EFT therapist is able to reframe each partner's behavior in terms of such cycles and in terms of the other partner's behavior. This is not reframing in the strategic sense of the term; the frame is not arbitrary, but arises from the increasingly elaborated emotional reality of the partners. As in the work of structural systemic family therapists such as Minuchin and Fishman (1981), each partner's behavior is constantly placed in the context of the other's response.

A voiced desperate desire for contact with the other would be framed here, not in terms of the deficits in the desperate spouse's character structure (she is too needy), or in terms of family of origin (she is seeing her partner as if he were her ungiving father), but in terms of the present relationship. Such desperation would most likely be framed as a reflection of the present distant position her partner takes in the relationship and her subsequent deprivation. The distancing behavior of the other spouse might then be framed as self-protection in the face of the other's angry pursuit, rather than as a reflection of indifference. Such reframes help partners to see how they unwittingly help to create the other's distress and resulting negative responses.

In EFT, each partner's behavior is placed not only in the context of the other's behavior and the pattern of interactions but, more specifically, in the context of intimate attachment, since this is the lens through which the EFT therapist views romantic love. *Interactional responses are framed in terms of underlying vulnerabilities and the attachment process.* Anger may therefore be framed as protest at the partner's perceived unavailability and a response to separation distress. Stonewalling on the part of a distant spouse, which is one of the behaviors associated with marital breakdown (Gottman, 1991), might be framed as this partner's attempt to regulate his attachment fears and to protect the relationship from escalating negative interactions. These reframes are not simply exterior labels placed on interactional responses by the therapist. They are most effective when they arise from the client's exploration of the own experience, how that client symbolizes his/her experience, and the process of interaction.

EXAMPLE

Therapist: So, of course, it's difficult to open up and show her who you are, when you feel sure she won't like who you are and will tell you that, or when you are sure she will be angry.

Gary: I just go numb. This voice says she'll leave me, like all the others did. I freeze, and she gets madder and madder.

Therapist: You freeze, 'cause it's like you've lost her already, almost. It's dangerous.

Gary: If I go real quiet, maybe it will stop and she'll calm down and cool off, if I'm still.

Therapist: If you stay completely still, the danger might pass? (*He nods.*) It's so scary, the idea that she will leave, you freeze and hide.

Gary: Yeah, and I know it makes her madder than hell.

Sue: I can't find you.

The frames proposed above, which place a response in the context of the other partner's behavior, the interactional cycle, and the nature of attachment, provide a metaperspective on the way the relationship is constructed, moment by moment. The couple engage in a process that demonstrates to them, in an immediate way, how the moves each one makes then pushes the dance in a particular direction, as well as how each is trying, in the best way he/she knows, to foster a safer attachment bond.

Restructuring and Shaping Interactions

The therapist directly choreographs new interactions between the partners to create new relationship events that will redefine the relationship. This is the most directive part of EFT and often the most dramatic. The therapist directs one partner to respond to the other in a particular way, encourages the expression of new emotional experience to the other, or supports each to state needs and wants directly. At these moments, the relationship moves into new and unfamiliar territory and each partner requires the direction and the support of the therapist.

The therapist may use such directions to do the following:

1. Crystallize and enact present positions so that they may be expanded.
2. Turn new emotional experience into a specific new response to the partner that challenges old patterns of relating.
3. Heighten new or rarely occurring responses, which have the potential to modify a partner's position.
4. Choreograph specific change events.

1. Enacting Present Positions so That They May Be Directly Experienced and Expanded

Key interactions that serve to maintain the structure of the relationship are focused on, highlighted, and enacted more and more explicitly. This is an immediate and powerful way to capture the impasses in a relationship interaction and make them accessible for modification.

EXAMPLE

In a 10-year relationship, in which the male partner holds back from commitment, insisting on keeping his own apartment, periodically breaking away only to reconnect after a few weeks in a highly romantic manner, he says:

Jose: I cannot quite make the leap you know. I like my tranquillity. Perhaps we should stop the sessions for a few months, that is the best decision, the only one I can make. You are so beautiful, please don't take this personally.

Marie: Well I know this leap, this getting closer, is hard for you.

Therapist: Jose, the decision is? Help me understand?

Jose: Perhaps if we have a few months apart, then I will feel the loss.

Therapist: The decision is to hold back, yes, (*He nods.*) to stay separate? (*He nods*) So can you tell her please: I'm not going to let you in, I'll let you come so far, but no further.

Jose: Well, I . . . I'm not sure. I don't think I can say it.

Therapist: Can you tell her: I'm not going to let you in. I never have. I've never let any woman into where she can really hurt me and I don't want to.

Jose: (*sighs*) Do I have to say this? This is sad.

Therapist: Does it fit for you. Perhaps I said it wrong?

Jose: No, I think it's right (*long silence*). It's hard to say. (*Therapist nods, agrees.*)

Therapist: I think it's important. You guys have been here, at this point, many times before. (*They nod.*)

Jose: (*looks at his partner*) I, I will not let you in. I've never let anyone in, (*He weeps*) never . . . no.

Therapist: Is there anything she could do to change this, Jose? She has been trying so hard for so long.

Jose: No, no . . . (*to his partner*) there's nothing you can do. I have to decide to risk.

The therapist may also ask the couple to replay specific, crucial interactions that seem to capture the essence of the negative cycle. The therapist extracts and lifts up a small significant part of the interaction, one that seems to present a microcosm of the relationship, out of the ongoing dialogue. For example:

Therapist: What was that there? Alison, you said, I hurt, and, Tim, you said, I disagree with that. This seems to happen all the time, doesn't it? You say, "I hurt," and then, Tim, you say, "No, you don't. I didn't do anything bad." Can we go back there? Can you tell him about your hurt, Alison?

2. *Turning New Emotional Experience into a New Response to the Partner*

This occurs when the therapist has helped an individual partner explore an emotional experience and a new synthesis of this experience has emerged. This new experience is then expressed to the spouse in a direct way. This is the first step to creating a new kind of positive dialogue and modifying partners' positions. Change in EFT comes not from a reprocessing of inner emotional experience, but from new dialogues that arise as a result of this experience. The therapist crystallizes this experience in interpersonal terms, that is, as it relates to the other spouse, using the client's own words as much as possible, and then asks the client to express this version to the other partner. The client usually complies, often modifying the message slightly to make it completely his/her own.

If the client cannot express his/her feelings to the other then this is focused upon and explored.

EXAMPLES

1. **Therapist:** So, can you look at her? Can you tell her, "I'm so afraid, I'm so afraid to risk reaching for you. I know you'll turn away."

2. **Therapist:** There seems to be this great longing. (*Client nods*) It's never really said. Can you let him know a little about that? About how much you long to just be held and comforted?

3. **Therapist:** So, have I got it right? Even in your anger you are still saying: "I want to give myself, to love you." (*Client nods.*) I protect myself with my coldness. I want to be safe and close too, but not on your terms. (*She nods again.*) Can you tell him this please?

3. Heightening New Responses

Here the therapist draws attention to and heightens any response that is outside of the usual negative pattern and has the potential to create a new kind of engagement. In the normal course of events, such responses might sometimes occur, but they tend to become submerged in the usual pattern of dialogue between partners.

EXAMPLE

Therapist: What just happened there? That was different. What was that like for you, Mike, to say what you just said?

Husband: Well, I guess it is a bit different, . . . maybe I was a bit different, it was like, like a risk, like coming out.

Therapist: Can you tell Joan that again, I think it was something like: "Don't tell me who I am, it pushes me away." (*The therapist summarizes and clarifies what was said and asks the person to enact this new response again.*)

4. Choreographing Change Events

As new emotional experience and new aspects of self emerge in therapy and attachment issues come to the fore, the therapist is able to facilitate interactions that more and more redefine the relationship in terms of autonomy/control and closeness/distance and create the basis for more emotional engagement and a more secure bond. The term "choreograph" is used deliberately in that, like a choreographer, the therapist has an overview of the dance and gives step-by-step direction and structure, but the dance is also the dancer's own creation and a vehicle for the expression of self.

There is a sense in which all of the interventions described above lead up to the events of engagement and bonding. Once these events take place or, alternatively, there is a clear definition of the relationship in terms of separateness, a new dance begins. All the new experience and new interactional moves that have evolved in the therapy session are synthesized here to redefine each partner's position and the bond between them.

In a typical blame/withdraw cycle, the two necessary shifts in position are the following: The withdrawn partner becomes more accessible, more emotionally engaged with himself and his spouse; the blaming partner moves from anger and coercion, asking for attachment needs to be met from a position of vulnerability. This invites contact and allows for bonding events where both partners can be accessible and responsive to each other. *In change events, a spouse explicitly takes a new position with the partner and this new position then elicits a reorganization of the interaction.*

The therapist keeps the interaction focused, curtailing detours and exits, directs and crystallizes emotional expression, and gently guides the couple in the direction of emotional engagement. Let us look at one brief example of an EFT therapist choreographing the continued engagement of a usually withdrawn husband, and the subsequent beginning of a softening in his critical spouse, culminating in a bonding event.

EXAMPLE

Mary: So why didn't you tell me you were so depressed? I asked you and you said you were fine, and then went off and tried to hurt yourself. You took all those pills.

Ted: Because I expected you to tell me to go and tell my therapist. I didn't believe you would understand.

Therapist: It would have been such a risk and you were already so raw, (*He nods*) but in fact it was her you wanted, not your therapist.

Ted: Sure it was. If I could have reached out to her and got comfort, that would have made all the difference, but I couldn't risk it.

Therapist: You couldn't bear the thought that she might reject you, so you gave up?

Ted: Yeah, and now I want her to (*therapist motions to him to direct his speech to his spouse*), I want you to climb down from your tank, stop solving problems and interrogating me, so we can be together, that's what I need. (*Mary looks away.*)

Therapist: What's happening, Mary?

Mary: I feel confused, I'm good at solving problems, it's my style. I don't know what to say.

Therapist: What happens for you when Ted says he needs you?

Mary: It feels good, but I don't know what to do. It's like I've lost my bearings. Do you think you need me more than your friends at work? (*Exit to old response of questioning spouse.*)

Therapist: Mary, can you tell him: "I feel confused."

Mary: Yeah, . . . it's hot in here, . . . if I can't problem solve, what does he want? (*Therapist looks at Ted.*)

Ted: I want you, . . . more than a problem solver . . .

Mary: (*weeps*) Well, that's it, . . . if I'm not the great director, the manager . . . it feels vulnerable. I'm not sure of myself here. (*Starts furiously rubbing her hands.*)

Therapist: This is strange territory, huh? (*Mary nods.*) You're uncertain, feeling vulnerable and knowing that Ted sees that. It's a little different, a little scary perhaps?

Mary: Sure, sure it is. I'm not as tough as everyone thinks I am.

Therapist: Can you tell him: It's scary to step out of that tank and be vulnerable.

Mary: (*to Ted*) It is. I'm unsure of myself here. Do you want that? I've never done that.

Ted: (*weeps*) I want us to be together (*cups his hands and clasps them together in front of his chest*), not you managing me. Can we? (*He is now emotionally engaged and asserting his needs with his wife.*)

Mary: I'll try.

Here the therapist not only helps one partner formulate new responses to the other, but fosters the creation of a new dialogue based upon these new responses. In the above example, the process went smoothly, but at other times the therapist may have to help the partners attend to, process, and acknowledge these new responses from the other spouse. After such an intervention, the therapist also makes explicit the new positions the partners are taking with each other and the implications of these new positions and dialogues for the relationship.

TECHNIQUES SPECIFIC TO DIFFICULT THERAPEUTIC IMPASSES

There are also specific techniques the EFT therapist uses in difficult impasses. These are:

1. Presenting diagnostic pictures and narratives of the couple's interactions and positions in a manner that makes the impasse explicit and confronts the couple with the consequences of this impasse for their relationship.
2. Conducting individual sessions to explore specific blocks in the therapy process.

Diagnostic Pictures or Narratives

Here the therapist paints pictures of the couple's positions and cycles and elaborates on the nature of the present process. In effect, it is as if the therapist says, "We are stuck here, aren't we? How can we move and what happens if we can't?"

The picture the therapist paints is concrete and specific. It is based on the process of previous sessions and the couple's own perceptions of this process. This graphic presentation of the present status of the relationship heightens the partners' sense of the impasse. It also presents them with a limited number of choices about the future nature of the relationship. Often this process results in a new risk being taken, or a new response given, that will break the impasse.

The most common form of impasse encountered in EFT seems to be when a previously less engaged partner is now available, but the other partner cannot bring him/herself to risk trusting and allow emotional engagement. The therapist might first recount the story of therapy up until the present time, then paint a picture of the present interactional patterns and describe how they place the relationship in neutral.

EXAMPLE

Therapist: So this seems right to you? We have come to the point where, Terry, you are really wanting to connect with Sarah. I see you inviting her to come and be with you, not hiding or trying to force her to come, but holding out your hands, yeah? (*He nods.*) And Sarah, you see it too?

Sarah: I guess so, yes, yes, he is. I know, he's different.

Therapist: But you're still, as you describe it, behind your wall. You're not sure you want to learn to trust him, is that it?

Sarah: I just wanted the fights to stop, and they have, really. I'm not sure about closeness, that's a whole other thing. Perhaps I want a more distant relationship than he does.

The therapist helps Sarah articulate her reservation about creating a closer relationship; for her, this is, as she described it, "bungee jumping." The couple can then talk about the consequences of staying where they are, in the impasse. The therapist's task is to present the choices that are available to them. It is important that the therapist not judge the appropriateness of their choices or impose values and choices on the couple. The couple have to decide what they can and will live with. This may be very different from the therapist's view of a good relationship or from one that the therapist might want for him/herself.

The essential nature of an impasse can sometimes be captured in a dramatic narrative. For example, a male partner suffering from posttraumatic stress disorder, was in crisis and becoming dangerously coercive and demanding with his wife. He was told a story that attempted to capture the emotional reality of, and the couple's positions in, the relationship. The story began: "Once upon a time there was a little boy, and he lived in a very scary cold place. The boy met a girl and asked her to hold him. She agreed because she loved the little boy, but her arms began to ache, and she asked to put him down for a moment. The little boy became terrified and believed she would leave, so he insisted that she hold him. In the end, her arms hurt so badly that she put him down. He was enraged and kicked her. Then, very reluctantly, very sadly, she left." This kind of narrative allows the partners to see the larger picture and can expand an obsessive focus on one aspect of the relationship. It is, of course, useful only if the couple are "caught" by the narrative and use it to reprocess their own situation.

Individual Sessions

Individual sessions, if used, are always balanced between partners. If one partner is given one, the other partner is also given one. In these sessions, experiential techniques are used to address specific emotional responses that seem to block emotional engagement in the marital sessions, or to focus intensely on problematic responses that undermine progress in the marital sessions. The therapist might focus, for example, on a partner's threats to leave the relationship (discussed elsewhere, Johnson & Greenberg, 1995), or explore responses (such as shame) that can inhibit risk-taking in the couple sessions, making it very difficult for one partner to ask the other to respond to attachment needs.

In addition to experiential techniques for reprocessing problematic reactions (Greenberg et al., 1993), an attachment frame and dialogues with attachment figures are actively used. With very self-depreciating partners who judge themselves unworthy of love, the therapist, for example, might use previous positive attachments to challenge this negative view of self. The therapist does this in the form of an imaginary encounter with this attachment figure. The client is asked to articulate, for instance, how his mother might see his present situation in his marriage and what she might say to him. He is thus asked to formulate, with the therapist's help, a more compassionate and accepting view of himself. Again, such techniques are useful only if the client becomes emotionally engaged in the process.

Individual sessions can also be useful when a crisis occurs that threatens to swamp the therapy process. For example, when the death of a parent results in a sudden withdrawal from the couple relationship, that threatens to undermine all the progress already made in marital sessions.

SUMMARY

The therapist in EFT acts as a guide, a process consultant, to the reprocessing and reorganization of emotional experience in relation to the partner, and to the reorganization of interactions in such a way as to promote emotional engagement and secure bonding. This is a powerful change process, involving an exploration of each partner's habitual ways of connecting to and engaging not only with intimate others, but also with their own emotions, attachment needs, and core representations of self. The purpose is to generate a corrective emotional and interactional experience of self in relation to other, and also to empower people to create the kinds of relationships they want in their lives.

In a typical session of EFT, the therapist might be focused upon the following activities:

- **Monitoring the alliance:** "I sense this process is difficult for you. Is there some way I can be more supportive?"

- **Reflecting secondary emotion:** "And, Sally, you get very angry when this happens because it feels like such a no-win situation. I understand (to the other partner) that to you, the anger seems to come out of the blue."

- **Reflecting underlying emotions:** "So, what it's like is, there is a kind of panic when he turns his back, is that right?"

- **Validating present responses:** "I think I'm starting to understand. For you, 'shutting down,' as you call it, is your natural way to cope. In fact, it has protected you all through your life, so when alarm bells go off, it just comes up as the only thing to do."

- **Validating newly experienced underlying emotion:** "It is very hard for you when you hear your wife say that you've disappointed her. You might seem impervious but, in fact, it's like a knife in your heart. It hurts so much that you go numb."

- **Evocative responding:**
  a) "What happens when you hear your wife talking like this, John? When she talks about feeling cornered and confined? How do you feel as you listen to her say this?"
  b) "What happened right there, Alan? Mary said that she has never felt taken care of in this relationship; then you closed your lips and folded your arms across your chest?"
- **Heightening:** "Can you say that again, Evan? Where are you? I can't find you." Can you look at her and say that again?"
- **Engaging in empathic conjecture:** "I'm not sure I quite understand. Is it like, if she doesn't desire me every day, I've lost her? That's the signal I rely on to reassure myself that she's still here, that she wants me. Is that it?"
- **Tracking and reflecting interactions:** "What just happened there, you said . . . and then you said . . . ?"
- **Reframing each partner's behavior in the context of the cycle:** "So this is dangerous ground for both of you right now. You feel that you have to protest; protest how distant Jim is, but actually that scares you, Jim. You see her as angry at you and that adds to your sense that you'd better find a place to hide, yes?"
- **Reframing each person's behavior in the context of attachment needs:** "When you do this, what you call ambush, it's like you have to get him to respond, to know that you do have an impact and that there is still a relationship, a connection, is that it?"
- **Restructuring interactions:** "So, can you tell her that, Tom, can you tell her, I don't know how to come and be close; I don't know how."

It is now time to turn from techniques to the process of therapy, in which these interventions are woven together to accomplish particular tasks at particular times.

4

ASSESSMENT—MAKING MAPS AND LISTENING TO MUSIC: EFT STEPS 1 AND 2

This chapter describes the first two steps in the EFT treatment process: the delineation of conflict issues and the identification of the negative interaction cycle that maintains the couple's distress and precludes secure bonding. Assessment is not separated from treatment here. The first two sessions are usually conceptualized as assessment. The therapist may choose also to conduct one individual session for each partner at this point. However, treatment starts with the first contact between couple and therapist.

GENERAL THERAPEUTIC GOALS

The therapist's general goals in the first sessions are as follows:

- To connect with both partners. To create an alliance where both partners feel safe and accepted by the therapist, and begin to have confidence that the therapist understands their goals and needs and will be able to help them.

- To assess the nature of the problem and the relationship, including its suitability for marital therapy in general and for EFT in particular.
- To assess each partner's goals and agendas for therapy and to ascertain whether these goals are feasible and compatible, not only in terms of the partners' individual agendas, but also the therapist's skills and the nature of the therapy.
- To create a therapeutic agreement between the couple and the therapist, a consensus as to therapeutic goals and how therapy will be conducted.

An agreement about therapeutic goals is not possible if, for example, couples have widely divergent and/or conflicting therapy agendas. In a couple where the husband has already left the relationship, but the wife has coerced him into seeking marital therapy in a desperate attempt to change his mind, the partners are usually advised to seek some kind of individual help. However, a few sessions of marital therapy can clarify the nature of the relationship, perhaps helping the still engaged partner to begin the grieving process.

Partners also occasionally come for therapy with agendas that the therapist cannot engage in—for example, the partner who is enraged that his wife will not conform to his demands and whose one agenda for therapy is to get the therapist to agree that his wife is mentally ill, thus persuading her to comply with his requests. There are times when the most therapeutic intervention is *not* to engage in marital therapy.

More specifically, there are contraindications for the use of EFT. These will be discussed in more detail in Chapter 9. EFT is not used, for example, where there is ongoing violence in a relationship, or where there is evidence that the exposure of vulnerability will place a partner at risk, as in the case of a verbally abusive husband who in the session unrelentingly demeans his partner and mocks her when she speaks of her suicidal depression.

PROCESS GOALS

If there are problems such as those mentioned above, they will emerge in the process of the assessment as the therapist follows the process goals outlined below.

- To begin to enter into the experience of each partner and sense how each constructs his/her experience of this relationship.
- To begin to make hypotheses as to the vulnerabilities and attachment issues underlying each partner's position in the relationship.
- To track and describe the typical recurring sequences of interactions that perpetuate this couple's distress and to crystallize each partner's position in that interaction.
- To begin to understand how the present relationship evolved and what prompted the couple to seek therapy. To hear the couple's story of their relationship.
- To begin to hypothesize as to the blocks to secure attachment and emotional engagement within and between partners and to explore these. Are they both wanting the same kind of relationship? Are they both committed to the relationship?
- To sense how this couple responds to interventions and how easy or difficult the process of therapy is going to be. Do they each take some responsibility for the problems in the relationship? How open and willing are they to take risks in the session? The level of rigidity in the enactment of positions and the reactivity of responses are noted.

By the end of the assessment, as the therapist turns towards Step 3 of EFT, he/she has a map of the typical interactions that define the attachment between this couple, a clear sense of their positions and patterns. The therapist also begins to have a sense of how these are experienced on an emotional level by each partner. He/she begins to sense the *tone* of the relationship, the music of the dance.

THE THERAPY PROCESS

What do the first few sessions of EFT look like? What is the usual process as a therapist guides the couple through the first two steps of therapy? Let us try to get an overview of a typical session by considering the questions that go through the therapist's mind as the first sessions evolve. They might be as follows:

- Who are these people? What does the general fabric of their life look like? The therapist gathers basic information.
- How did they decide to come for therapy at this particular time?
- How does each of them see the problem in the relationship. Can they sustain a dialogue about their views or are their views radically different and/or rigidly held?
- Does each of them see strengths in the relationship? What keeps them together? How do they describe each other? As they tell their stories, what kinds of problematic interactions are described and how did they attempt to deal with them?
- How do they view the history of the relationship and understand how they originally connected?
- How does each of them present his/herself and his/her own history to the therapist? Does each person's story suggest any particular attachment issues and/or problems?
- How do the couple generally interact in the session. If asked to interact around a particular topic, how does the dialogue evolve? What messages are conveyed by each partner's nonverbal responses?

The couple generally experience these sessions as relatively intense and emotionally engaging. They are encouraged to tell their story of marital distress, describe their fights and problems, as well as their positive moments, and to dialogue about difficult topics. The therapist, while allowing the couple the space to describe the last fight, to state their points of view, or tell how their differing approaches to conflict are typical of their family histories, also asks directive questions and focuses the session on attachment issues, emotional experience, and interactional sequences.

In a couple session, so much occurs on so many different levels that the key issue, even for an experienced therapist, is where to look or what to pay attention to in the crowded landscape of facts, feelings, incidents, and interactions. In first sessions, partners usually describe key pivotal relationship incidents that define how the relationship is for each of them and contain implications about how the self is defined in relation to the other. They also enact powerful interactional sequences, sometimes heightened by the therapist, that capture the essential quality of the relationship. These moments are like personal and interactional landmarks in the landscape of the marriage and help to clarify the therapist's emerging picture of the couple's predicament. These landmarks are always characterized by a shift toward more deeply experienced affect. Particular note is taken of how, in the process of describing or enacting such incidents, one partner defines the other, labeling his/her experience and character, and also how partners define themselves in relation to their partner. To give the reader a sense of these kind of incidents, some examples are given below.

Personal Landmarks/Incidents

Such incidents have attachment significance often not understood by the other partner. They are continually referred to in the interactions, often as ammunition in an argument. They cannot be forgotten or left behind and they cannot be resolved in the present emotional climate of the relationship.

- A wife recounts that her parents wanted a boy and told her she was ugly and retarded. The real punch, however, comes when she tearfully recounts that when her husband told his family about her, he described her as a good woman, from a good family, even if she was not very pretty. As she recounts this, she weeps, while her partner smiles and minimizes the incident, thus fueling her anger and her alienation from him.

- A wife tells how her husband refused to accompany her to a potentially traumatic medical appointment at the hospital because his friend had called and asked to see him.

- An apparently very reserved man, who presents as very rational and detached, insists that for him there is no problem in the marriage. His wife is alienated by his accommodating reserve. He then begins to describe how he once, ten years ago, had had a very brief affair during which his lover once told him that he was physically beautiful and desirable, and he begins to weep uncontrollably.

All these incidents are like a door opening onto the partners' experience of their marriage. They also provide clues as to the nature of their pain and their sense of self in relation to the other partner. Such incidents can be seen in attachment terms as abandonments and betrayals, and/or as ways into the attachment wounds and longings of these partners. The EFT therapist will stay with and validate these experiences, helping the client elaborate on them and their significance for the relationship. The therapist will also use them in future sessions as a reference point for a partner's emotional experience in the relationship.

Interactional Landmarks

In the first sessions, interactions occur that vividly demonstrate the positions of the partners and their negative cycle.

These are noted and may be reflected back to the couple. They can also be expanded and elaborated as part of the assessment process. This expansion must be particularly respectful and carefully done since it is early in the therapy process and only a preliminary alliance exists between the partners and the therapist. For example, interactions may occur where one partner dominates or effectively controls the interaction. The therapist notes how the other partner responds, as well as how and when the more controlling partner acts in this way:

- As when a husband tearfully states that he cannot go on with the very extensive infertility treatments that his wife is insisting on. She then cuts him off and explains in a calm, controlled manner that she cannot help it if he is infertile. He must, therefore, continue with the agreed-upon procedures. The husband then looks resigned and visibly withdraws from the conversation.

- As when a wife describes how humiliated she feels when her spouse criticizes her in front of her family. He states that if she would improve her behavior, for example, by doing her chores more conscientiously, he would not have to criticize her. She cries at this point, while he continues to point out to her that even here in the session her communication skills are deficient. The wife then begins to plead with her partner to be less of a perfectionist.

- As when one partner accuses and threatens, while the other remains calm and detached. The first partner increases the tenor of the accusation and the other definitively labels this partner as sick or deficient in some way. The first partner then weeps and withdraws. After a short pause and perhaps a change of topic, this pattern occurs again.

These kinds of incidents may just be noted by the therapist, or they may be focused on, depending on the process of the session. For example, the wife who did the chores imperfectly might be asked to continue to try to get her husband to hear her distress, with the therapist providing support to both of the partners. As the couple try to complete this task, they demonstrate the rigidity or relative flexibility of the present interaction pattern and how the responses of each partner contribute to the pattern.

Interactions also usually occur that demonstrate the quality of contact and support in the relationship and the blocks to such contact and support. One spouse will become vulnerable, for example, and the therapist will note the other's response or lack of response:

- As when a woman cries over the death of a newborn child and states that she feels alone in her grief. She then asks her husband if he ever feels this way. The spouse looks at the ceiling and states that crying will not bring the child back and there is no point to it. His wife then attacks him for all the ways she sees that he disappoints his children by his long absences from home.

- As when the wife states that her partner is emotionally crippled and cannot feel. Later in the session, he weeps. The therapist asks the wife, who is looking out the window, what is happening with her as her husband weeps. She states that she does not believe in, or trust, his response and sees him as manipulating the therapist.

- As when a highly intellectualizing and withdrawn spouse breaks down at the end of a first session and, with tears in his eyes, states that he does not know how to show his wife that he loves her very much and that she is the source of his happiness in life. His wife, who has previously complained bitterly about not being loved or feeling important to her spouse, indignantly attacks him and states that she is not any hothouse flower and feels demeaned by his tone and comment.

The couple usually show the therapist, who fosters and heightens their interactions, not only the power and affiliation aspects of the positions they take in relation to each other, but also how in a negative cycle the position taken by one spouse recursively evokes the position taken by the other. The speed, automaticity, and the rigidity of the cycle is noted. Couples will vary in *how aware* they are of the cycle, *how compelling* the cycle is, whether they have *any ways of exiting* and reinitiating a different form of contact, and *how much of the relationship it has encompassed.* Often, couples wait until the cycle can be more accurately described as a *spin*, before they seek out a therapist. The word spin captures the speed and self-perpetuating, absorbing nature of the negative cycle. This cycle may then absorb and color every element in the couple's relationship.

INDIVIDUAL SESSIONS

As part of the assessment process, the EFT therapist often conducts an individual session with each of the partners, usually after the first or second conjoint sessions. The purpose of these individual sessions is:

1. To foster the therapeutic alliance with each partner.
2. To observe and interact with each partner in a different context, one in which the spouse is absent.
3. To obtain information and check hypotheses that are difficult to explore in front of the spouse. For example, the therapist can seek information on commitment level, extramarital relationships, or previous personal attachment traumas that impact the present relationship. The therapist also can explore how each partner perceives his/her spouse; such uncensored key perceptions of the other may be useful in later therapy sessions.
4. Such sessions allow the therapist to refine his/her impression of the underlying feelings and attachment insecurities that influence each partner's interactional

position and to begin to articulate these insecurities with individual partners.

The issue of the therapist being stuck with secrets that undermine his/her therapeutic effectiveness does not seem to arise here. In the collaborative partnership of the alliance, if information arises that is likely to undermine therapeutic attempts to improve the relationship, such as an ongoing emotional involvement with another person, this is explored in terms of the client's goals for the therapy sessions and effects on the marital relationship. The therapist then requests that this information be shared with the other partner in order to meet the goals of therapy. He/she helps the individual explore any fears or reservations about such disclosures. The therapist also helps this partner share the information with the spouse in the next session.

In the first sessions, assessment and treatment are intermingled. If first sessions are considered as treatment, what are the therapeutic processes and interventions that usually occur? The following section will discuss this in the format that will be used in all the following chapters to discuss all nine steps of EFT. This format includes:

- The *markers* (points of intervention) and *tasks* in the therapy process.
- Therapeutic *interventions*.
- Couple *change processes* and how these processes are understood in EFT, as well as the *end state* of such processes.

THERAPEUTIC PROCESSES

Therapeutic Markers

A first session in couples therapy can be compared to suddenly finding oneself in the middle of a play, without knowing the plot or the characters. One of the first steps in a therapy model is to formulate what the therapist notes and responds to in the session. A marker is a point in therapy where a particular type of expression or interactional event signals to the therapist an emotional processing or interactional problem, or an opportunity to intervene in the above. The occurrence of particular markers suggests particular tasks and interventions to the EFT therapist, which lead to particular client performances/activities and contribute to change in the session. Markers in EFT are prototypical reactions, both emotional responses to the partner and interactional events that define the relational experience and the structure of the couple's marriage. They are signals to the therapist to pay attention and to intervene.

The kinds of markers that usually occur in the first sessions are both intrapsychic and interpersonal.

Intrapsychic Markers

1. As one partner tells his/her story of the relationship and the problems in the relationship, strong emotional responses interrupt the narrative. At this point, partners usually exhibit nonverbal signs of strong affect—crying, flushing red, turning away, biting the lips, clenching the fists, and the flow of the narrative or dialogue is interrupted.

    The task here is to focus on and acknowledge the affect, thereby creating a secure base in the therapy session for such experiencing.

2. As one partner tells his/her story, the lack of emotion is very marked. Dramatic and often traumatic events are reported from a detached stance, as if they had happened to someone else. The incongruity between what is being said and the manner in which it is reported—in a sense, emotion that is conspicuous by its absence—grabs the therapist's attention. The task here is to explore the lack of engagement in personal experience and what this signifies concerning the couple's engagement in, and definition of, the relationship.

3. During moments of intense affect, partners articulate beliefs concerning themselves, the other partner, or

their relationship that appear rigidly organized and/or
destructive in the present context. These beliefs are
often stated as definitions of identity. The self, the
other, the relationship or relationships in general are
defined and declared to be constituted in a particular
way. The partners often convey the meanings that they
have given to key relational events in terms that pre-
clude the possibility of change or the development of
any new perspective or information. The task here is
to reflect and elucidate such beliefs and begin to frame
them as part of the destructive cycle that controls the
couple's relationship.

4. Particular attachment issues are identified, but are not
owned, or are responded to in ways that block resolution of such issues; for example, a wife blames her partner for being a "workaholic," but does not seem willing
to focus on her own sense of abandonment and loss.
The task here is to begin to focus on such issues and
frame them as central to the ongoing problem in the
couple's relationship.

Interpersonal Markers

1. In the first sessions, the therapist particularly notes
position markers, that is, comments or responses that
appear to define power/control and closeness/dis-
tance in the relationship. These markers occur in
dialogue between the therapist and each partner, in
the dialogue between the partners, and in the stories
of the relationship that each partner tells. The task
here is for the therapist to get a clear picture of the
position each partner takes in relation to the other
and each partner's perception of and emotional responses to such positions.

2. The therapist also notes *negative* cycle markers. By far
the most common cycle in distressed couples is some
form of pursue/criticize, withdraw/avoid. However,
withdraw/withdraw cycles where both partners are

relatively disengaged and volatile attack/attack cycles are also seen. In withdraw/withdraw cycles, the story the couple tell often makes it clear that this cycle has developed from the pursue/withdraw pattern; by the time they come for therapy, however, the pursuer has also begun to disengage and withdraw.

The couple tell the therapist about, and enact, the manner in which the positions they take with each other interconnect to create negative self-reinforcing patterns in the relationship. The therapist tracks and clarifies such cycles. The task is to become clear about what the cycle is and to frame it in such a way that the couple find it relevant and true to their experience. They can then begin to integrate it into their way of thinking about the relationship. Individual responses are placed in the expanded context of the cycle.

3. The therapist particularly notes the way the partners interact when there is an opportunity for positive contact, particularly how that contact is blocked. This illustrates how the attachment insecurities of each partner are played out in the interaction. The task is to note if and how the couple make positive contact, and to note and explore exits from such contact; as when one partner reaches for the other and the other rapidly shifts to an accessible position. If such contact is created in the first sessions, the task is to focus on it and acknowledge it as part of the strength of the relationship.

INTERVENTIONS

The interventions the EFT therapist is most likely to use at this point in therapy are:

Reflection

In early sessions, reflection often consists of empathic reflections of each partner's experience of the relationship and of the sequences of interaction, positive and negative, that characterize the relationship.

EXAMPLE

Therapist: So, help me get this straight, Rob. You're saying that you once found Yvonne's more distant, quiet style alluring and mysterious, but now it frustrates and enrages you and usually ends up with you questioning her, or what she experiences as "badgering." Is that it?

Validation

This is particularly crucial in the first sessions. The therapist conveys the message that the partners' emotions and responses are legitimate and understandable, and their responses are the best solutions they could find in the light of each partner's experience of the relationship. This proactive acceptance of each person is essential to a strong alliance and to the process of EFT.

EXAMPLE

Therapist: I think I understand, Marie. You are talking about feeling so desperate, so desperate to know how Rob feels about you, that threatening to hurt yourself with those pills was your way of trying to get relief from this dreadful doubt. The doubt that he doesn't care, or wishes that he could be rid of you. I understand that for you, Rob, it doesn't feel like this. You feel tricked and enraged, like Marie is pulling your strings.

Evocative Reflections and Questions

These interventions are always offered in a tentative and respectful fashion; however this is especially true in the first few sessions when the therapist is learning about the relationship and the alliance is not yet formed. The therapist focuses upon unclear or emerging aspects of experience to clarify how each partner perceives and experiences the problem in the relationship and to identify the interactional positions and cycles. However, this is done with deliberate care and respect. Any issues concerning the partners' engagement in the process of therapy, their reservations, anxieties and doubts, are also the focus of such reflections. The task here is not so much the active reprocessing of experience, but rather the accessing of each person's experience of the relationship.

EXAMPLE

Therapist: So what is it like for you to hear Mary talk about you in this caring way?

or

So what has it been like for both of you to talk to me? You have shared some very difficult and painful things.

Heightening and empathic conjecture are used much less in beginning sessions, although the therapist may summarize partners' responses in an evocative or dramatic manner to crystallize the cycle and/or each partner's experience of the relationship. The partners are also *explicitly* encouraged to correct the therapist and help the therapist understand, if they feel that he/she is in any way painting a picture that they cannot relate to, appears inaccurate, or makes them uncomfortable.

Tracking and Reflecting Interactions

At this stage, the therapist focuses especially on typical behavior sequences that seem to define the relationship and reflect attachment issues. This is an essential part of identifying the patterns of interaction. The sequences of interaction are then plotted from the narrative presentation of the relationship, from the description of specific incidents, and from observation of interactions in the session.

EXAMPLE

Therapist: So how it goes, then, is that a lot of your relationship is taken up with Fred feeling left out and getting
"feisty" and "prickly," and you refusing to be "picked
on," as you put it, and moving even further away. Is that
it? Just like what happened here a moment ago, he reached
over and poked you and you brushed him off and moved
your chair away.

Reframing

This intervention may be used in the first sessions, but on a
relatively superficial level. Even in the first session, the therapist may begin to frame one spouse as deprived, for example,
and the other as needing to protect the self through distance.
However, this depends on whether the partners express their
experience in a way that is amenable to such formulations.
Such reframes can be incorporated as part of the description
of the cycle. In a general sense, the moment that the couple
make contact with the therapist, the kinds of questions he/she
asks and the focus taken begin the process of reframing the
couple's problems and issues. However, the central task at the
very beginning of therapy is to engage the couple in therapy
and to begin to grasp the intrapsychic and interactional struggles that structure the relationship.

EXAMPLE

Therapist: The moving away is your way of standing up
for yourself, protecting yourself, from his "poking," yes?
And for you, poking is your way of saying, "I'm here, here
I am, let me in, see me." Is that it?

COUPLE PROCESS AND END STATE

The desired outcome of the first sessions in EFT is that both
partners feel understood and acknowledged by the therapist.

They begin to feel safe in the session and to have confidence in the therapist as a person who will respect them and as a professional who can understand the struggles in their relationship. The therapist instills hope in the partners by structuring the session so that each is heard, by validating each partner's experience and strengths, and by conveying directly that, for every couple, close relationships are a struggle, but a struggle that the therapist expects to be able to help them with. The summary at the end of the first sessions always includes a description of the struggles they have already engaged in and won, even if the only apparent one of this kind is that they have decided to come for help. By the end of the first session, the therapist is also creating an alliance where he/she is an accepted partner in the creation of a more loving relationship.

If the result of the first sessions is that the therapist does not recommend EFT, then the couple is given feedback and a diagnostic picture, which usually includes a description of their interaction cycle and a summary of how each seems to experience this relationship, as well as the reasons why EFT is not being offered. Other forms of help are then discussed and referral sources offered, whether they be individual therapy, groups for addictions, learning to overcome anger problems, or other forms of couple oriented interventions such as divorce mediation.

During the course of the first sessions, the couple usually travel from uncertainty about the process of therapy to more comfort and confidence in it; from anxiety about the therapist to a sense of being accepted by the therapist and being able to rely on him/her for help; from a sense of confusion and desperation about the relationship to the beginning of a sense of hope and agency; from a sense of stuckness in dead-end interactions, such as fights about who is to blame for the present state of the relationship, to a sense of new possibilities and discovery; from a constricted picture of the relationship and a narrow focus on its impact on the self, to an expanded view of the cycle and how it keeps both partners trapped and helpless.

A transcript from a first session of EFT may be found elsewhere (Johnson & Greenberg, 1992). A training tape of EFT also shows the process described in this transcript (Johnson, 1993).

5

CHANGING THE MUSIC:
EFT STEPS 3 AND 4

"I feel so small, so naked when I ask. So I make myself bigger, pushier."

"It sure works, you terrify the hell out of me—I go hide."

This chapter describes Steps 3 and 4 in the therapy process. These are: accessing the unacknowledged feelings underlying interactional positions and reframing the problem in terms of these underlying feelings and attachment needs.

At this point in therapy, the first task of the therapist is to access the music of the couple's dance, that is, the primary emotions that are usually excluded from individual awareness and not explicitly included in the partners' interactions. The second task is to use these emotional responses, and the attachment needs reflected by such responses, to expand the context of the couple's problems. The problem is framed in terms of the way the couple interact and the emotional responses that organize such interactions.

This chapter presents the markers and tasks, therapeutic interventions, couple change processes, and end state of this part of therapy. As previously stated, the steps of therapy do not occur in a set linear fashion; rather, each step tends to be integrated into the next step or steps, so that the EFT therapist will continue to access emotion during the process of Steps 4 to 9, building on the framework constructed in Step 3. Later sessions and steps of EFT, therefore, contain elements of previous steps, which are then integrated into the tasks of the present session. When underlying emotions are first accessed in Step 3, they are related to the position each partner takes in the relationship. Later, this step is integrated into Step 5, where such emotions are experienced more fully and related to the way each partner perceives self and other in the relationship. In Step 7, these emotional experiences form the basis of the expression of needs and wants.

Each partner also progresses through these steps at a different rate. Usually, one partner will take the lead and begin in Step 3 to move ahead of the other. This is often the less engaged and more withdrawn partner. If both partners are withdrawn, it is usually the one who is most easily engaged in therapy who moves ahead.

Accessing emotion in Step 3 of EFT does *not* consist of the following:

- Reiterating the past emotional experience of the relationship, to blame the other or justify the self
- Ventilating negative emotions in the hope that uninhibited expression will diminish such responses
- Labeling one partner's emotional responses to teach the other partner to behave differently
- Discussing emotions from a cognitive distance or, to use an analytic term, from the point of view of the observing ego

Accessing emotion here involves the following:

- An active engagement in, and focus on, emotional experience occurring in the here and now
- An expansion of that experience so that the experience can be differentiated
- A reprocessing of experience that involves a process of discovery and creation, so that new aspects of experience are encountered

- A symbolizing of that experience in terms that are relevant for the way this partner responds to his/her spouse

MARKERS

In Step 3, the therapist intervenes in the following instances:

- When one of the partners expresses the reactive secondary emotions that make up a large part of a distressed couple's interactions. This is usually anger or frustration that is expressed in the process of blaming the other or justifying the self. The task here is first to acknowledge and validate these secondary responses, but then to engage with the client in the process of exploring specific experiences and eliciting the emotions that are disowned, discounted, or avoided. This can occur as the partner tells the therapist the story of the relationship and the distress in the relationship, or as he/she recounts an incident that is particularly relevant to how he/she perceives the relationship. It can also occur as a couple interact in front of the therapist in the session.
- When one of the partners exhibits nonverbal behavior in response to the other partner that is noteworthy due to its incongruity, intensity, or effect on the interaction. As a wife complains and weeps, for example, a husband taps his foot and frowns with apparent impatience. His wife then looks at him and lapses into silence. In another couple, a wife states that she is going to leave the relationship and the husband begins to laugh and talk about possible summer holidays. The task here is for the therapist to slow down the process of interaction and focus attention on the emotion implicit in the nonverbal behavior.
- When a partner begins to explore his/her emotional responses in the session, and to encounter a new, alive sense of how he/she experiences this relationship, or

begins to symbolize this experience in a new way, but
exits from this process rapidly, often becoming caught
up in the negative interaction cycle with the partner.
The other partner may also discount this experience and
elicit the usual fight/flight response, which then takes
precedence over the beginning exploration. The therapist's task is to redirect the process in the session back
to the exploration and help the partner engage in it
more fully.

• When the couple exhibit the interactional cycle that has
been identified in Step 2. The partners themselves may
now identify the interaction as part of the cycle or the
therapist may comment on it. The task, now, is to focus
on one person's position in the interaction and how this
person experiences the other partner and his/her own
compelling emotions in this interaction.

On one level, each couple have their own idiosyncratic ways
of interacting and experiencing the relationship. Indeed, the
process of therapy has to be a process of discovery for them,
the discovery of the unique, particular aspects of their inner
and outer worlds and how they create their own distress and
happiness. For the EFT therapist, however, certain relationship positions can be predictably associated with particular
underlying emotions, even though how these emotions are experienced, processed, and symbolized will vary with each individual.

This predictability is enhanced by attachment theory, the
theory of relatedness that forms the basis of EFT. So spouses
who take an angry, pursuing, critical position in the interaction often access panic and insecurity when the therapist directs them to explore their underlying emotions. Attachment
fears of abandonment and/or rejection will surface. On the
other hand, the partner taking a withdrawn position is more
likely to access a sense of intimidation and incompetence related to being unable to please his/her partner, as well as a
paralyzing sense of helplessness. This arises from not knowing

how to respond to the partner in a way that will elicit positive attachment responses, or at least curtail the negative cycle.

INTERVENTIONS

Before stipulating interventions, it is important to stress the HOW, the manner in which interventions are presented, since this is particularly crucial at this point in therapy.

The nonverbal behaviors of the therapist are an essential part of accessing underlying emotions. These behaviors convey acceptance and help to create a secure base from which each partner can explore his/her experience. They also either help or hinder the client's ability to focus on and process his/her experience. The power of these nonverbal behaviors cannot be overemphasized. They often make the difference between an effective and non-effective intervention; between the client engaging in his/her experience and simply labeling and/or avoiding it. When an EFT therapist is eliciting underlying emotions, he/she will usually be exhibiting the following:

- An open stance towards the partner, often leaning forward
- A slower speaking pace than is usual, with longer pauses
- A lower, softer voice than is usual
- Relatively simple, concrete words, often images, often using the clients own words

In effect, the therapist models an intense focus on a particular aspect of the partner's experience and invites the partner to follow and to emotionally connect with the experience in a more intense way.

The interventions that the EFT therapist is most likely to use at this point in therapy are discussed in the following sections.

Validation

Validation is crucial at this point in therapy. Reflection is used and is a basic intervention in all steps, but in Step 3 it is more of a prelude to validation and evocative reflection and questions than a main intervention. The importance of the therapist's validation of emotional states becomes clear when one considers that one of the primary blocks to engagement with one's own emotional state is automatic self-critical cognitions about the unacceptable, inappropriate, and even dangerous nature of particular emotions. Expectations that certain emotions and their expression will be unacceptable to others also block such engagement. The message to be conveyed here is that the therapist sees each partner's emotions and responds to them as valid, legitimate, understandable human responses. This provides an antidote to the self-critical stance many clients take with regard to their emotions and encourages deeper involvement in and exploration of them.

The therapist's explicit valuing and acknowledgment of each partner's experience builds a secure base in therapy, allowing partners to express themselves more openly and risk the other partner's disapproval in the session. The EFT therapist will reflect a feeling and validate it as a first step in encouraging partners to enter more fully into their emotional experience.

EXAMPLES

Therapist: I hear that for you what Ellen calls your "constant gestapo questioning and analyzing" is like an urgent search—search to try to find out why you never seem to get really close to her. As a scientist, it is a natural way for you to respond. You're trying to find the answer, trying to find the key to solve the problem that is torturing you, the problem of how lonely you feel in the relationship.

or

Therapist: It seems like it is somehow demeaning or embarrassing for you to talk about how you need comfort from Mark. You somehow seem to feel that this is something that you should not need, yes? It's hard for you to talk about that? Sometimes we are brought up to believe that being strong means not needing others, and then it's hard to admit when we find that we do. It sounds like it takes a lot of courage for you to talk about this.

Evocative Reflections and Questions

These interventions are designed to open up and expand each partner's emotional experience of the relationship. The therapist follows the client's experience and focuses upon the partial, tentative, or "in process" edges of this experience, which have a poignant and/or emerging quality. This intervention first invites the client to stay in contact with a particular experience and then, to process it further. As this occurs, new elements then emerge, which reorganize the experience. The therapist is a partner in this engagement, this processing and reprocessing, so that this experience unfolds and evolves in the session. As stated previously, the therapist may begin with a focus on a cue or stimulus, such as bodily response, or an impetus to action, or any awareness that arises spontaneously as part of the processing of that experience. The therapist may simply repeat certain phrases, offer an image or metaphor, or ask exploratory questions.

EXAMPLES

Therapist: What is happening to you, Jim, as your wife describes how she sees you and how disappointed she has been in this relationship?

Therapist: What is it like for you, Paul, to always be on shifting sand, careful, cautious, vigilant, on eggshells. How does that feel for you?

Therapist: What's happening for you, as you right now describe the "massacre," as you call it?

Therapist: What's happening for you as you throw up your hands and say; "I can't comfort a raging bull."

Heightening

The therapist intensifies, crystallizes, and encourages the couple to enact key problematic as well as new, reprocessed emotional responses, that organize interactional positions. Maintaining a consistent and persistent focus is also a way of heightening responses or interpersonal interactions and messages.

EXAMPLE

Therapist: Ted, you have said lots of things here but I guess the part that stood out for me was the phrase, "It burns me." It was when you were talking about Jenny's disapproval. "It burns me." It's so painful for you not to be able to please her that it burns. Burns are unbearably painful. (*Ted begins to cry.*)

Empathic Conjecture

In this intervention, the therapist encourages one of the partners to process his/her experience one step further by expanding on the present experience, using inferences drawn from the therapist's experience of this person or his/her relational context, and incorporating the therapist's perspective on marital distress and intimate attachments. The therapist may offer a formulation of the person's experience that adds a new element, or puts elements together in a new way, hopefully crystallizing this experience or symbolizing it in a new way. The more "in contact" with this person the therapist is and the more empathically immersed in his/her experience, the more poignant and relevant such inferences will be to the client and the more likely he/she is to adopt and use them.

The alliance in EFT is such that, if the therapist's comments are not useful or relevant, partners will usually correct the therapist or simply reject the formulation. In marital therapy, such inferences are open to immediate corrective feedback, either from the experiencing person, or from the other spouse, or from the therapist's ongoing observation of the couple's relationship. Inferences that are too far away from the way clients' frame their own experience will not be adopted and, if offered continually, will damage the alliance, since partners feel misunderstood and discounted by the therapist. Ideally, these inferences are also offered in a tentative manner that encourages the client to correct them and are *only one short step ahead* of the client's own awareness.

In EFT, these inferences are often used to crystallize partners' attachment insecurities and fears and to relate such fears to specific elements of the partner's behavior, that act as triggers for such fears. These inferences are best made in a simple, concrete, and evocative way, with the same nonverbal therapist responses suggested earlier.

EXAMPLE

Therapist: When you say: "I'm like a kid. I hate it, but I have to ask," and then you stare at the floor, I get the sense that there's a shame in that for you, in asking? (*Client nods.*) and a sadness perhaps?

Tim: Yeah, Oh yeah, I want not to ask and ask.

Therapist: For her to come in and get you.

Tim: Yeah, that's it. I really want that, but . . . .

Therapist: So it's hard to ask, and when you have to, you resent it?

Tim: Right, so when I do ask, I guess I ask kind of pushy. I say "Kiss me now."

Therapist: You sort of feel small when you ask, so you make yourself bigger, pushier maybe?

Tracking and Reflecting Patterns and Cycles of Interaction

In both Steps 3 and 4, the therapist places each partner's emotional responses, as they are accessed, in the context of the other partner's behavior and the couple's cycle. This tends to validate each person's responses and begins to create a more process-oriented view of exactly what the problem is in the relationship. Step 2, the identification of the cycle, is then integrated into Steps 3 and 4.

As emotions are accessed, they are related to the cycle and to each person's attachment needs. The description of the cycle is, in turn, expanded to include each partner's compelling emotional responses. The context of the cycle stresses the legitimacy of each person's responses and feeds back into the further accessing and reprocessing of emotion.

In Step 4, the couple are ready to adopt the cycle and the newly accessed insecurities that feed into the cycle as *the problem.*

EXAMPLE

Therapist: So when he withdraws, like he did just now, when he went silent and turned away, that just makes you "go hot," as you put it. It's alarming. *(She nods.)* You can't reach him, so, usually, now what would you do?

Helen: I'd verbally clobber him. He can't ignore me.

Glen: And then I'd withdraw more. It's the pattern we've been talking about. It's so hard to step out of.

Reframing of the Problem in Terms of Contexts and Cycles

This is both a general intervention in EFT that occurs throughout therapy (the problem is always placed in the context of the cycle) and a specific step in treatment (Step 4). Here the therapist summarizes the process of Steps 2 and 3 and explicitly formulates the problem as the positions the couple take in the pattern of interactions, the negative cycles that have taken over their relationship, and the compelling emotions that organize each person's responses. This replaces the general formulations of the problem that the couple came in with, such as "communication problems," or specific formulations that helped maintain marital distress, such as "the problem is that she thinks we have a problem."

EXAMPLES

Therapist: Yeah, the swing-and-run pattern is kind of running things right now, but I think you guys are starting to take it apart, bit by bit.

or

Therapist: So this pattern has kind of taken over your relationship. It gets in the way of all the closeness you used to have together and keeps everyone's emotions churning, so both of you are sensitive and raw. Is that it?

June: Yeah, and I understand how it keeps me hot and heavy, looking for trouble and pushing him away. So he hides more, but (*to spouse*) you get mad too.

Jim: I get most angry when I'm most afraid you'll leave. I think mostly we are both scared to death, and that throws everything off.

COUPLE PROCESS AND END STATE

The lack of open communication, particularly around attachment issues and emotional vulnerabilities, *constricts not only the couple's interactions, but each partner's experiencing and processing of his/her own affect.* Distressed partners hide their vulnerabilities not only from each other, but from themselves as well in that even experiencing such feelings becomes problematic and/or foreign to them. Most partners, therefore, experience Step 3 of EFT as risky and anxiety provoking. They face at least four fears. They are:

- The dragon of self-criticism, as in, "I hate this part of me; it's pathetic."

- The dragon of testing out the process of revealing aspects of self that they are unsure of and uncomfortable with, as in; "I never felt this before, maybe I'm going crazy."
- The dragon of facing the anticipated negative response of the other spouse, as in, "She'll laugh at me, worse still, she'll despise me. She won't want me to touch her."
- The dragon of unpredictable change in a distressed but predictable relationship, as in, "I'm lost. I feel like I don't know you. Who have I been with all these years and what do I do now?"

The other side of the experience is that they find tremendous *relief* in being able to process and understand their own emotions and their relationship patterns, and a sense of *efficacy* when they begin to vividly experience how each person unwittingly creates the relationship cycle (as in, "If I created it, maybe I can make it different"). There is also relief in being able to acknowledge responsibility in a context where this does not incur a sense of shame or deficiency. Partners make comments such as; "I've never said this to anyone, hell, I've never even let myself feel this way before, but this is the way it is with me." The other partner's reaction to this is often puzzlement, disorientation, and disbelief, as in; "I don't believe this. I've never heard you speak like this before. I feel like I don't even know who you are."

In this process, the predictable support and direction of the therapist provides a secure base for continued exploration. For example, with a partner expressing the disbelief mentioned above, the therapist would reflect and validate such responses. This disbelief and even distrust and testing of the "new" partner are not seen as neurotic collusion, as in analytic models, but as a natural response to new and disconcerting perceptions of the spouse.

To maintain this secure base, the therapist has to be able to change focus rapidly from accessing one partner's feelings to exploring the impact of this on the other and supporting the other, or from helping the partner deepen his/her exploration of such emotions to processing the other partner's negative responses and including them in the process. For instance, when an observing spouse expresses skepticism, the therapist might state, "I see that this must be strange for you to hear this, different from how you have experienced your husband all these years. So it's a little difficult for you to take. Maybe you are too angry to hear what he is saying right now, but it seems important to me that he gets to say what is real for him. So I'm just going to help him do that for a moment, and then we will talk further about what it's like for you to hear this."

It is during Step 3 that each spouse's attachment issues emerge and begin to be clarified, and that these issues first become an explicit part of the dialogue between the couple. In Step 4, these issues and the interaction patterns that block emotional engagement are framed as the problem. The couple adopt this frame and make it their own because it springs out of their immediate emotional experience.

The underlying emotional experiences are often different for male and female partners. Female partners more often identify lack of connection and deprivation of contact as the main factors in their distress, whereas male partners more often identify feelings of inadequacy and incompetence as the main elements. In similar fashion, emotional distance in relationships has been found to be related to women's health status, whereas disagreements and overt aversiveness have been found to be related to men's health (Fisher et al., 1992).

This is also the time when attachment betrayals or crimes, that is, traumatic incidents that have damaged the nature of the attachment and actively influence the way the relationship is defined in the present, are explored and clarified. For example, a small current incident where one partner is disappointed may become an enormous issue because it evokes a key incident in the past, where one partner experienced traumatic abandonment, rejection, or betrayal at the hands of the other, or even from another important attachment figure. As the emotions underlying interactional positions are processed, these incidents come alive in the session and begin to be dealt with in a constructive way.

As partners access and begin to reprocess their emotions, their key cognitions, schemes, or working models concerning the perception and definition of self and other begin to surface in an alive and vivid way. This process continues and becomes more intense in Step 5. This is a process of discovery for the partners, rather than the disclosure of already formulated and familiar views. Fears about the unlovable nature of the self, for example, begin to be accessed in this step.

By the end of Step 4, the couple has formulated a coherent and meaningful picture and/or story of the patterns that define their relationship, as well as of how they create them. This picture has been co-created with the therapist, but it is their story and they own it because it fits with their emotional experience. The self, as experienced in relation to the other, has already expanded and the presentation of self begins to shift to be congruent with this experience. The withdrawn partner is now talking in the session about his paralysis in the face of his wife's criticism, rather than just going numb and silent. His wife is still angry, but not as actively hostile as before and is beginning to talk of her hurt.

This constitutes a *De-escalation*, one of the designated points of change in EFT. This is a first order change (Watzlawick, Weakland, & Fisch, 1974) in that the positions the partners take are somewhat more fluid, but the way the interactions are organized has not basically changed. The other designated points of change are when the withdrawn partner moves to a position of *Re-engagement* and asserts the terms of this re-engagement, and when the previously hostile spouse allows a *Softening*. These will be described in a later chapter. As mentioned previously, one partner is generally one step ahead of the other.

By this point in therapy, the perceptions of the other partner have also begun to shift, as that other partner reveals more of himself/herself. For example, the withdrawn partner is perhaps now perceived not so much as indifferent or uncaring, but rather as withdrawing as protection from the enormous impact of the other's actions. The therapist frames the negative cycle as the result of the enormous impact the partners have on each other and their attempts to cope with this. This is reassuring for partners and they are usually willing to adopt this frame, not only because they experience their partner differently in the session, but also because it is aversive to experience an attachment relationship as they have up to this point, that is, as one where they appear to have no emotional impact on the other partner.

Withdrawers also usually react well to the discovery that their partner's hostility is not the result of random aggression, but is rather a desperate response to their own withdrawal. The power of withdrawal seems to be a particularly novel idea to many partners. An attachment frame helps to elucidate the aversive impact of withdrawal, since, in this frame, withdrawal defines the person as inaccessible and unresponsive. The fact that the withdrawn partner seemingly cannot be reached or moved threatens the other's attachment security in a compelling way. In short, for both partners, the other now seems less dangerous and less difficult to influence than at the beginning of therapy. The more hostile partner's behavior might then be perceived less in terms of "She is trying to destroy me." and more in terms of "She will do anything to get me to respond to her."

This shift in perception is particularly enhanced by the fact that the therapist directs partners to interact on the basis of the newly accessed emotions. Thus, a wife not only witnesses her partner elaborating on his emotional experience with the therapist, she also experiences him turning to her and sharing that experience, telling her, for example; "I'm so scared of disappointing you that I hide most of the time." This is not only new information of a powerful nature. It also redefines the relationship as one where this kind of message/contact is possible and is, in and of itself, a new enactment, a new performance that changes the play.

By the end of Step 4, the partners are engaged in a new kind of dialogue about emotions, attachment issues, and cycles, and how these all go together, and are beginning to be emotionally engaged with each other in the therapy sessions.

6

FACING THE DRAGON: EFT STEPS 5 AND 6

And she said,

> "I'm the maiden in the cave. Your fears—all this trust stuff, are like a dragon blocking your path to me. Am I worth fighting the dragon for? How can you turn away and let the dragon win?"

This chapter describes Steps 5 and 6, promoting identification of disowned needs and aspects of self and integrating these into the relationship and promoting acceptance of the partner's experience and new ways of interacting. Step 5 is the most intrapsychically focused step in EFT. The experiential concept of changing in the process of therapy into more of what one is, rather than trying harder to be what one is not, is relevant here. As the self is experienced in a different way, the presentation of self changes, so the man who once cringed and placated now becomes angry and assertive. Step 6 involves the therapist helping the other partner to begin to accept and incorporate this new presentation into his/her view of the partner and to be responsive to the partner's new behavior in the interaction.

There is a sense in which Step 5 is a watershed in the therapy process. The first four steps lead up to Step 5 and Steps 6 to 9 build on the processes inherent in Step 5, using these processes to restructure the partners' interaction. In research on the process of change in EFT (Johnson & Greenberg, 1988),

the partners who allowed themselves to become intensely involved in their emotional experience were the ones whose
relationship changed the most in therapy. This intense
involvement is the essence of Step 5. The intense engagement
with one's own emotions allows the therapist to begin to facilitate a new kind of emotional engagement with the other
partner.

In Step 5, previously unformulated or avoided experience
is encountered, claimed, and congruently expressed to the
partner. This, in and of itself, expands each person's experience of the relationship. The withdrawn husband, who generally avoids the anxious feelings elicited by his wife's
comments, and so ends up avoiding his wife most of the time,
now fully experiences and states his fear of her criticism. In
doing so, he owns his strategies for dealing with this fear ("I
hide and shut you out.") His revelation, to his wife and to
himself, elicits new feelings in him as to his position in the
relationship ("I don't want to be so afraid; I don't want to have
to hide, I want to be accepted.") and presents a new image to
his wife. This revised image then has the potential to evoke a
new kind of response from her. Step 6 is, in fact, concerned
with helping the partner deal in a constructive way with this
new behavior (for example, revealing the self as afraid) and
new image. Specifically, in Step 6 the therapist contains any
effects of the initial discounting of the partner's new response
by the distressed other, supporting the other in his/her confusion at encountering this "new" spouse. In effect, the therapist
throws his/her weight behind the change in pattern.

The word "disowned" in the description of Step 5 is worth
stressing. In Step 5, partners own and take possession of their
emotional experience of the relationship and this tends to *empower* the experiencing partner. How does this occur? First,
the process of Step 5 orients the individual to his/her needs
in the relationship, and second, *newly accessed emotions also
elicit new action tendencies.* For example, a withdrawn husband professes his fear and, in the process, accesses and expresses his unfulfilled need and longing for acceptance. This
then also begins to elicit emotions that do not fit with his usual

hiding and avoiding, such as anger, and these emotions spark a desire to take a stand and state his desires.

In the description of Step 5, disowned needs are referred to, rather than simply disowned emotions. The implication here is that accessing the emotions underlying interactional positions also accesses the attachment needs that are so often the referent for such emotions—for example, accessing a sense of abandonment panic also accesses the innate need for contact and reassurance from the attachment figure. *It is in Step 5 that attachment longings and desires begin to be clearly articulated.*

The description of Step 5 also refers to aspects of self, since the recognition of such primary emotions and needs is intricately connected to the definition of self. The most dramatic emotions that arise in Step 5 are connected to each partner's sense of self, particularly the lovableness and worthiness of self. The process of Step 5 can then be seen as one in which less known and accepted aspects of self are integrated into the person's experience and into the relationship. For example, allowing oneself to connect with, and expose to another, vulnerabilities that are usually denied or brushed aside *expands the sense of self and the person's interactional position.* As a result of the powerful emotions that arise here, emotions that are intricately linked to the person's sense of identity and attachment security, core definitions of self and other become available and open to modification. Such modification occurs through new interactional experiences with the therapist and, much more importantly, with the partner.

As Bowlby (1988) suggests, emotional communication provides vital information for constructing and reconstructing working models of self. However, if attachment theory is not familiar to the reader, one could also think of the links between self-definition and relationship definition in constructionistic terms; a perspective that is currently very much part of systemic therapies. According to this perspective, significant others are the principal agents in the maintenance of subjective reality and particularly in the confirmation of that crucial element of reality called identity (Berger & Luckmann,

1979). Symbolizing and presenting a previously disowned aspect of self to a significant other and then enacting that aspect of self in the relationship expand and redefine the nature of that self. This is particularly likely to occur if the other partner can accept these new aspects of his/her mate and if the effects of this enactment are positive for the relationship.

MARKERS

In Step 5, the therapist intervenes when the following occurs:

- The emotional responses accessed by a partner in Step 3 are experienced or referred to by the client in the session. These emotions are now more easily identified and symbolized by this person and related to his/her interactional position in the couple's cycle. For example, when the therapist asks a withdrawing partner what is happening for him, he now replies in a congruent manner: "I just give up. I'll never make it with her, I feel small and scared. So then I back off, go away." The task here is both to validate the emotion and the action it evokes, which is to withdraw and protect the self, and to help the partner further differentiate this experience and to own it.

  These emotions are most often idiosyncratic versions of fear, helplessness, and despair. As this differentiation process continues, the way the emotion is experienced and understood, the experiencer's judgments about him/herself for feeling this way, the view of the partner implied in the experience, and the usual way of coping with this experience, within the person and within the relationship, all become clear. This process is not an analysis or discussion of these elements. The person is immersed in the experience and these elements emerge as the experience evolves.

- A partner begins to explore, in a new and alive way, his/her underlying feelings, but is interrupted by the partner, or exits from the process into abstract cognition or general descriptive comments. The task is for the therapist to redirect the process and, if necessary, block the other partner's interference, thus encouraging a more intense involvement in the emotional experience.

In Step 6, the therapist intervenes when the following occurs:

- One of the partners reaches a sense of closure or synthesis of his/her underlying emotion with the therapist and is able to clearly relate this experience to habitual responses to the other partner. The therapist then requests that this person share this synthesis with the other partner and he/she does so, in an engaged manner. The focus in this sharing is on self, not other. The task in Step 6 is to support the other partner to hear, process, and respond to this sharing, so that this new experience can become part of, and begin to reshape, the couple's interactions.

    There is no reason why the observing spouse should be particularly open to, or trusting of, this shift in the way this partner presents him/herself in the relationship. On the contrary, such partners have had years of disappointment and of negative experiences, which mediate against such responsiveness. If the therapist is not present, this lack of responsiveness to such sharing becomes a potentially aversive experience for the partner who is opening up. This results in a reinitiation of the negative cycle and a return by this partner to his/her more constricted position in the interaction. From a systemic point of view, the therapist promotes and expands this shift in the pattern of interactions, this new kind of dialogue, so that it is not simply inundated by, or subsumed in, the more established pattern, but in fact begins to reorganize that pattern.

    This step almost always begins with the therapist asking the observing partner, "So what is it like, what happens for you, when your partner talks like this and says . . . ?"

INTERVENTIONS

Reflection and validation of emotional experience, and the interactional responses they evoke are a constant part of the EFT therapist's interventions and also operate here. At this point in therapy, however, other interventions come to the fore and for this reason they are focused on here.

Evocative Responding

The therapist focuses upon the emerging but unformulated aspects of a partner's emotional experience and helps this partner to vividly grasp this experience, by unfolding and expanding it in the here-and-now of the session. The therapist uses vivid, specific, and concrete language, particularly images and metaphors, to assist the person in encapsulating his/her experience.

EXAMPLES

A. Expanding the felt sense of an emotional experience with questions and reflections.

Therapist: What is happening for you Jim, as you look down and say, "It's scary, to tell her who I am"?

Therapist: You're saying it's disappointing, Mary, is that right? (*She nods.*) It's so painful to hope that he is going to be there and then, just when you need him most, you can't find him. You get that sinking feeling in the pit of your stomach that you spoke about (*she nods*) and then . . . What does it feel like?

Reflection and question come together here to put different elements of the person's experience together, in her own words, and then invite her to experience more of it.

B. Expanding the context, the cue for the emotional experience.

Husband: Right about now I want to run and hide.

Therapist: This is scary, right now. (*He nods.*) What happened? What did you see?

Husband: It's the look on her face. She isn't going to believe me, no matter what I say. I can't win.

Therapist: The look on her face?

Husband: Yes, her raised eyebrows, it's like, "Yeah, right bud, tell me another one." Forget it.

Therapist: You were trying to reach her. Is that okay, (*he nods*) and she raises her eyebrows, and you feel . . . ?

Husband: Crushed.

Therapist: Crushed, crushed and defeated, like you want to run and hide.

Husband: Yeah.

C. Expanding the formulation/meaning of the experience and how it organizes the person's responses to the other.

Wife: I can't bear it, I feel so sad. How dare you say these things to me! (*She exits from the sadness into anger at her partner, who has just told her that she doesn't accept the caring he offers.*)

Therapist: You feel so sad about what he said, that the way he experiences it is that you can't accept his love.

Wife: I don't know what he is talking about. (*quieter*)

Therapist: Something happened here. Something happened that was "unbearable" for you, is that right?

Wife: It's like he's saying that it's my fault that I don't feel loved.

Therapist: Ah ha, you feel angry, like he is blaming you (*she nods*) for feeling so unloved, (*she starts to cry*) so sad, so alone, and that's unbearable.

Wife: Yes, and I don't like that feeling, that sadness,

Therapist: How does it feel, that sadness?

Wife: Like I'm a little helpless kid, snivelling, I won't be spoken to like that. (*angry voice*)

Therapist: Where did the sadness go? (*She laughs.*) You sound angry now. (*She nods.*) Does that feel better than feeling like a sad little unloved kid?

Wife: Yes. It feels safer to be angry (*She laughs.*) It's like then I don't feel so sad and helpless. It's better.

Therapist: You feel safer, bigger, being angry? So what happens to the sadness?

Wife: He doesn't see it, and it feels better.

Therapist: What would happen if you let yourself just feel sad?

Wife: I . . . I . . . might fall apart. I'd weep forever and he wouldn't like that.

The therapist then goes on to evoke and explore the grief and loss implicit in "I'd weep forever." The implications for the cycle are clear here; the wife's anger, as well as her need to protect herself from her own feelings of sadness and from her husband's feared rejection, narrow down her part of the interaction to angry complaining, which in turn evokes his withdrawal.

As can be seen from these examples, questions and reflections run together as the therapist tracks the person's experience and invites him/her to explore it. Simple techniques such as repetition also refocus the process on the more important elements, in this case the client's sadness. The therapist also replays the process, going back to the emotional experience and elaborating on it. Images that partners formulate in this process are particularly helpful and can be used in later sessions to evoke the emotional experience associated with them.

HEIGHTENING

The therapist heightens the emotional responses to make them more alive and present, and so facilitate the clients' engagement with them. The therapist also heightens the interactional position that reflects (and continually recreates) these responses. Heightening is a way of helping partners fully experience and resonate with their emotions, and a way of creating a powerful experience in the session; which will then influence behavior outside the session.

Heightening Emotion

EXAMPLE

Wife: It's like I don't belong.

Therapist: You aren't part of the family, part of his life?

Wife: Right. I'm all by myself.

Therapist: All by yourself, there is no one beside you, no one to hold your hand, to support you.

Wife: (*She cries.*) I'm not important. We went on a walk and he was playing with the dog and he didn't even notice that I turned back and went into the house.

Therapist: He didn't notice that you had left. You weren't there (*she nods and cries*). What did it feel like when you went into the house? You didn't matter, you were insignificant (*she nods*).

Wife: Like I don't exist.

Therapist: Like you are invisible?

Wife: Yes, the invisible wife. (*To partner*) You don't see me.

Therapist: So it's like you're saying, after a while it gets so I feel like I don't exist here, I'm nothing to you.

There is a sense in which all the interventions in EFT heighten emotion, simply because of the focus on emotional responses and the validation of such responses. Here, however, there is a deliberate attempt by the therapist to make the experience more vivid and to capture the considerable significance it has for the person and the relationship. This does not affect just the experiencing partner, but has great impact on the other observing partner, who hears this partner not just saying new and different words, but actually being a different way—that is, experiencing deeply and in a manner that pulls for a more compassionate, caring response.

Heightening Present and Changing Positions

This intervention encourages partners to own not just the emotions underlying their interactional positions, but also the positions themselves, which are reflections of these emotions and also ways of regulating them. A position that is consciously and actively taken and experienced as legitimate is already different from the exact same position occurring as an automatic response to the other's actions in which the associated emotions are only dimly sensed.

As mentioned before, Step 5 is a watershed in the EFT process. It includes owning present experience and the problematic position that reflects that experience. It also lays the groundwork, by expanding emotional experience and expression, for new positions to emerge in Step 7.

Heightening the Enactment of a Present Problematic Position

EXAMPLE

Therapist: Can you say that again Pete, "I don't want to trust you, some part of me would rather die than ask for your help. I've promised myself I'd never give anyone the power to really hurt me again."

Heightening the Enactment of an Emerging New Position

EXAMPLE

Therapist: How did you feel about what you just did, Pete?

Pete: You mean risking, risking showing her my softer side, my longings? (*Therapist nods.*) Fine.

Therapist: You feel strong enough to do that now, to take that step, to reach out to her. (*He nods.*) Can you tell her what that was like for you, risking, going against the voice that tells you to protect yourself and reaching for her?

EMPATHIC CONJECTURE

This is used in Steps 5 and 6, to expand and clarify experience in Step 5, as well as to frame any difficulties partners might have in responding to the emerging changes in their spouse in Step 6.

In Step 5, this intervention ascribes meaning or creates a contextual frame for the immediate, compelling emotional experience that is occurring in the session. If this frame does not fit exactly with the client's experience and enrich that experience, the client corrects the therapist and the therapist acknowledges and uses the correction. Often, the therapist adds just one element to the formulation of the experience or places it in the context of attachment needs and fears.

While insight might be part of this process as it evolves, this is not the goal of this intervention. The goal is to deepen the person's connection with his/her emotional experience and to allow this experience to further unfold.

Empathic conjecture is probably used more at this point in EFT than at any other. It is perhaps useful to state here that empathic conjecture is *not*:

• Replacing one set of cognitive labels for another

- An abstract intellectual summary of experience
- Instruction to the client as to a better way to be or view things
- An attempt to create insight into self or other

Correctly used, empathic conjecture arises from the following:

- The therapist's empathic immersion in the client's experience in the here and now.
- The therapist's sense of the relational context, the positions and patterns, and the intrapsychic experience that is usually associated with such positions and patterns.
- The theoretical framework of EFT, which assumes that attachment theory is a powerful framework for explicating adult intimacy.
- The therapist's own emotional processing which provides clues as to how others might be experiencing a specific situation.

An ideal conjecture is respectful, tentative, specific and just one step ahead of the experience of the client as the client is formulating it. It often focuses upon attachment fears, not just fears concerning others' responses, but also fears concerning the nature of self. This focus on fear makes sense when one considers that fear, in particular, constricts both inner emotional processing and interpersonal engagement, thus narrowing the range of interpersonal responses.

Empathic Conjecture in Step 5

EXAMPLE

Therapist: So, when you come home early, as you drive to the house, you have this image that you will find Walt making love to someone else? (*Norma nods.*)

Norma: I will catch him. (*angrily*)

Therapist: Betraying you. (*Norma nods.*)

Walt: I have never even thought of such a thing in all my life, why would you even think I could do such a thing?

Norma: You are not making love to me!

Walt: You won't let me anywhere near you. You frost me out. Otherwise I sure would. I love you. (*Norma weeps.*)

Therapist: What's happening right now Norma? (*She stares at the floor.*) Something touched you? You were angry and then you wept.

Walt: Whenever I say I want her, love her, she weeps. There is a chink in the armor and then she goes silent.

Therapist: Is that right Norma? Is it hearing Walt say that he loves you that touches you?

Norma: (*edge in voice*) I don't believe he wants me. (*Walt sighs.*)

Therapist: But just for a moment, what he said touched you?

Norma: (*defiant posture*) I guess so.

Therapist: It touched you to hear him say he wanted you, and you wept, part of you wants that, even though another part doesn't believe him. (*She nods.*) Would you like to believe him?

Norma: Of course, but it's never happened, never.

Therapist: It's never happened that someone has really wanted and valued and cherished you, and there is something really sad about that. It's worth crying for, (*she nods*). One part of you wants to believe him and one part tells you to give up, stop being stupid and protect yourself, look hard enough and you will find him betraying you, yes? He will let you down.

Norma: Yes, I don't want to want it . . . , to think . . . perhaps . . . , and then . . .

Therapist: To let yourself long for that love, only to have your hopes dashed again. You shut the longing down and stay tough, yeah?

Norma: I don't feel the longing, only the anger, I don't even care if I'm that important to him.

Therapist: Is that right? It's not worth crying about, being important to someone, being special enough for Walt to fight for?

Norma: I've never felt special to anyone. I've given up on it. Everyone lets you down.

Therapist: You can't trust anyone. (*She nods.*) You won't give anyone the chance to let you down again. You're vigilant.

Norma: That's right, always watching, a voice says, "It will happen again, even with Walt, it will." (*Clenches her fists.*)

Therapist: The voice says, don't even think of trusting him, its a fool's game, right? Be on your guard. Come home early, who knows what you might find. You came home early to find what you are most afraid of?

Norma: (*Closes her eyes.*) The fear is so strong.

Empathic Conjecture in Step 6

EXAMPLE

Therapist: Walt, what is happening, as you listen to Norma talk like this?

Walt: I feel lots. I think, it's not fair, I'm unjustly condemned, I can't prove to her that I'm not like that, it's futile. I don't deserve all this testing and suspicion.

Therapist: Ah ha, you're indignant and hurt maybe. (*He nods.*) Can your hear how difficult it is for Norma to even think of trusting you, of letting her guard down.

Walt: I hear it.

Therapist: What happens for you when you hear it?

Walt: I feel sad. She's so wounded, and afraid . . . just like me !

Therapist: Can you tell her ?

Walt: I see you're afraid. How can I show you that I won't betray you ?

Therapist: You want to know how you can help her be less afraid? (*He nods.*) Ask her.

A special form of conjecture, a disquisition, is sometimes used in Step 6 to normalize any negative responses to the other's new experiencing and emerging new position.

Disquisition in Step 6

EXAMPLE

Therapist: I understand that it is difficult for you to take such a risk and have Mary respond angrily, but for many partners who have been frustrated and hurt in the relationship, perhaps for a long time, it's very hard to respond when their partner begins to open up and take risks. Some people can't believe it or are afraid to believe it. Some people want the other person to feel some of the same hurt they have felt over the years. It makes it hard for you to keep risking, but it's also really hard to take it in when our partner does something different. It's a whole new story, almost like having a new partner, kind of strange, disconcerting. But I don't know if any of this is relevant to you, Mary, 'cause you have your own feelings and realities.

As stated before, Step 5 is the most intrapersonally oriented of the EFT treatment steps. Step 6 also focuses on individual responses, so the more interpersonal interventions are less prominent at this point in therapy. The reframing of interactional responses in attachment terms is part of the empathic conjecture intervention, but is used more as an intrapsychic than interpersonal intervention here. The interpersonal intervention, restructuring interactions, does occur in Steps 5 and 6 in that new experience that arises here is used as the basis to create new kinds of interactions. This process continues and is even more central in Step 7. It is interesting to note that even in the most intrapsychic steps of EFT, inner experience is still related to and used to restructure interactions. The EFT therapist is always standing on the edge of inner and outer, and playing with how each reflects and creates the other.

RESTRUCTURING INTERACTIONS

The therapist choreographs enactments of present positions that are now more explicitly, consciously, and actively taken and shapes those interactions to include new elements from the newly synthesized experience arising in Step 5, thus turning new emotional experience into new interactions. In Step 6, the therapist monitors the responses of the other partner to this new experience/expression and, if necessary, choreographs less constricting and/or more accepting responses.

Step 5

EXAMPLE

Therapist: So can you tell him Norma, "I am so afraid. I don't even let myself even hope, even long for your love anymore. I wrap my prickles (*Norma's word*) around me and wait and search for evidence, for you to betray me. I only let myself touch that longing for a moment."

Step 6

EXAMPLE

Therapist: Can you tell her Bill, "I'm too angry to hear you right now. I'm not going to acknowledge the risks you're taking."

COUPLE PROCESS AND END STATE

What happens in Steps 5 and 6 from the couple's point of view? If therapy is going according to plan, many different elements are interacting on many different levels. Although one partner generally enters Step 5 before the other, both partners' experience a similar process. This process is characterized by the following:

- An intensification and heightening of the emotional experience accessed in Step 3. This involves a process of differentiating and symbolizing this experience as it occurs. With this process comes a recognition of the significance of this experience for the self in relation to the other: "I have to protect myself. Who is going to take care of me? No one ever has and I gave up on it long ago. When we first got together, I hoped that you . . . but . . . "

- An owning of that experience as belonging to the self (not created by the other). As the person inhabits and lives out of the experience, he/she also owns the action tendencies, the impulses arising out of this experience, which have organized this person's interactional position and helped create the negative cycle in the relationship: "I'm so scared. I guess if I do risk reaching for you, I do it in a kind of qualified, indirect sort of way and the minute it looks like it might go wrong, I run. Most of the time, I guess, I'm behind a wall. No wonder you can't find me."

- The expanded experiencing and owning of the experience and the person's position in the cycle also involve
the accessing of core self concepts or models, associated
with the intense emotions that arise here. These concepts
seem to arise naturally in this kind of emotionally loaded
interpersonal situation where there is also a therapist
to provide safety. Experiencing the pain of how one is
negatively defined in an attachment relationship accesses a partner's sense of self in a clear and poignant
fashion that allows for active exploration and eventual
reformulation: "So I say to myself, what do you expect?
You're not good at this love stuff. I feel about this big,
(making a small space between thumb and forefinger).
I'm a hopeless case. I can't even ask her anymore. I'm
some sort of freak in this emotional stuff, you know. I
know this, so when she starts to tell me she's disappointed, as if I didn't know I was disappointing her, I
can't stand it. So I start yelling."

All of the above allows for a reprocessing of primary emotions related to the sense of self in relation to the other; in
this process, the experience of the connection with the other
develops and changes. Specifically, key wishes and longings
inherent in the emotion begin to emerge and to be articulated.
They can then be worked with in Step 7. Before this stage,
partners usually have difficulty articulating what it is they
want, perhaps because they do not feel entitled to the response
they need, or because their desires are not clear to them or are
too painful to hold in awareness. They are also reluctant to
ask, since asking would place them in a position of vulnerability with their partner.

From an attachment point of view, attachment behaviors
begin to change at this point in therapy as the emotions that
organized them are reprocessed. A previously withdrawn
spouse becomes more accessible and also becomes more assertive, taking some control over how the relationship is defined and how he/she is defined within it. The models of self
and other, accessed as "hot cognitions" in this process, are

available for reformulation. Interactional positions are more actively taken and start to shift toward more accessibility and contact. Attachment fears and insecurities are reprocessed and become a recognized part of the interaction, rather than controlling the dance from behind the scenes.

In terms of change events, Step 5 is crucial. It forms the foundation for Withdrawer Re-engagement for one partner and Softening, for the other. These events are discussed in more detail in a later chapter.

What happens here from the point of view of the observing partner who is often a step behind the other in the EFT process and observes the other as he/she goes ahead into the process of Step 5?

First, this partner sees his/her spouse *being* different. The word being is used deliberately in that this partner sees his/her spouse engaging in an intense exploration of his/her emotional experience, rather than simply acting differently. It is understandable that, when asked, couples identify a changed perception of their partner as the crucial change element in EFT. The way the spouse is perceived expands and becomes less rigidly organized. Old, set ways of viewing the other person are challenged by new experience. A partner, who has never wept cries and a partner who is never angry rages. This not only provides new information about this partner, but also fosters a sense of connection, a sense of shared common humanity between partners, that may have been lost in years of alienation and conflict. Partners speak of being touched, being moved in a new way, when witnessing their spouse's emotional reality. It may evoke compassion or, at the very least, curiosity.

Second, this observing partner is also engaged by the other in a very new kind of dialogue. It may not necessarily be more comfortable, and at first it may even seem to be more dangerous than the usual negative, but predictable, cycles that the couple engage in. This new dialogue begins not only to impact the emotions, but to challenge the interactional position of this observing partner. On a very concrete level, the experiencing partner who is immersed in the Step 5 process may appear significantly less dangerous than before. Therefore, the need for strong defenses against him/her is suddenly less obvious. This other partner may also begin to take a more assertive position in the relationship, whereas previously he/she had reacted in a passive manner. This can be frightening and/or very reassuring to the observing partner. In particular, the new dialogue contains the possibility of intimate contact and the observing partner is then in the position of having to respond to this, usually finding that his/her response is ambivalent, at least at first, even if he/she has been struggling for such contact for years.

Third, the observing partner also hears the other take responsibility for the position he/she has taken in the relationship, and for his/her part in the way the relationship has evolved. This tends to undermine a blaming stance towards the other and encourages this observing partner to join in taking responsibility for how the relationship has evolved.

All of the above applies whichever spouse leads in the process of therapy and enters Step 5 first. When the second partner reaches Step 5, it sets the stage for new bonding events, which usually occur when this second spouse engages in Step 7. As stated in Chapter 1, the order and independence of the steps in the change process is exaggerated here, in the interests of clarity. The evolution of the increased responsiveness of the usually withdrawn partner and the increased openness of the usually critical partner are intertwined and reciprocally determining. The reduction in hostility of the critical partner invites the other's approach; the reduction in the distance of the withdrawn partner encourages the other to risk and ask for what he/she needs. This process occurs throughout therapy. Most often the withdrawn partner leads in the process, but in some couples the more critical spouse may take the lead and reach Step 5 before the other partner, or both may enter the steps almost simultaneously.

Step 6 involves the crucial evolution of a new kind of dialogue between the partners and requires that, as these partners go through this experience, the therapist stay with them, track their experience, and support them. A recording of these observing partners' reactions at this point might sound something like this: "Is this real? Can he really be feeling this? Why haven't I seen this before? He is playing games. I'm not sure if I can, or want to, trust this. He is sad, now I feel sad too. Should I let myself feel this way? I'm not going to let down my guard just like that. It feels good to know he isn't indifferent, but is he really scared? Perhaps he can open up and then, then what, am I going to risk it again? Hope again? Not yet." If the relationship has been very adversarial, the first response is often some version of, "I don't believe this for a moment" or "go tell someone who cares."

Step 6 has, then, an *intraspsychic component*, that is, helping the observing partner process his/her partner's new responses and respond to them, and an interactional component, that is, structuring a new dialogue, including the new elements now present in each partner's experience of the relationship. The observing partner is encouraged to explore any negative responses to his/her spouse and to express them directly, as, "I'm still too angry to hear you and I'm not sure I want to believe you." As with the other steps, this step evolves over the course of several sessions, with the therapist fostering new and positive contact between the partners whenever possible. The experiencing partner may be framed as needing this observing partner's help in staying more engaged and risking more in the relationship.

As the experiencing partner stays out of the negative cycle and continues to construct a new position for him/herself in the relationship, the other begins to be confronted with his/her own difficulties in becoming more accessible and responsive. It is often the case that the first partner entering Step 5 and then Step 7 evokes the other partner's insecurities and pulls this partner into the owning of his/her fears and insecurities, that is, into entering Step 5 for him/herself. A now accessible and potentially responsive partner challenges reservations that this observing spouse may have about connecting with the other, confronting this spouse with his/her own unwillingness to risk and trust.

At this point, a certain amount of testing may be part of the therapy process and indeed may be necessary before this partner can begin to respond to the changing other. Such testing is reflected, validated, and placed in the context of the cycle. This encourages both spouses to stay engaged and to tolerate the anxiety that a new way of interacting generates. For the observing spouse, the process in Step 6 begins with a focus on the experiencing partner and evolves to a focus on his/her own ability to respond to this partner's new involvement in the relationship. For the experiencing spouse, Steps 5 and 6 expand this partner's emotional engagement in the relationship. This engagement then becomes alternative to behaviors associated with the negative cycle, such as avoidance, withdrawal, or angry coerciveness. The second time through Step 6 is usually brief and uncomplicated, whether it involves the now re-engaged, previously withdrawn partner responding to the softening of the more critical partner or, as occurs less frequently, the softened critical partner responding to the increasing engagement of the withdrawn partner as this partner enters Step 5.

In the event that the observing spouse becomes so distressed by the emerging changes in the relationship that he/she escalates the negative cycle, and the usual ways of dealing with these reactions mentioned above do not seem to have the desired effect, an individual session for each partner can be initiated. This is discussed more fully in the clinical issues section, in Chapter 9. Occasionally, key incidents in the history of the relationship, experienced as attachment traumas, reemerge in Step 6, blocking the observing spouse's ability to trust and respond to the other's new behaviors. An exploration of these critical attachment incidents or "crimes" can evoke the observing spouse's own deepest fears and hurts—that is, it can prime this person's own entry into the process of Step 5.

7

EMOTIONAL ENGAGEMENT: EFT STEP 7 AND CHANGE EVENTS

"It's hard for piglet and superwoman to be close."

"I need you to help me hold back the dark."

This chapter deals with Step 7 of EFT, facilitating the expression of needs and wants and creating emotional engagement. Step 7 involves the last stage of the process in which new emotional experience and expression are used to change interactional positions and so restructure interactions. It is at this point in therapy that key change events associated with successful outcome in EFT occur. The completion of Step 7 for the less engaged partner results in the change event, Withdrawer Re-engagement. For the other, more critical partner, this is a Softening event, in which this partner is able to ask for contact and comfort from a position of personal vulnerability. In addition, as the second partner reaches the end of this step, powerful new bonding events occur. These events heighten the developing emotional engagement between the couple and construct a new positive cycle. This cycle becomes as self-reinforcing as the original negative cycle and fosters a more secure attachment between partners.

It is the processing of emotional experience in Step 5 and the subsequent interactional events in Step 6 that lead into the statement of needs and wants in Step 7. This statement, made as it is from an empowered, accessible position, constitutes a shift in interactional position, which, and in turn, challenges the other partner to engage in the same process. The processing of emotion in Step 5 leads naturally into a heightened awareness and expression of needs and wants, just as an awareness of hunger leads to a clear desire for food and an expression of that desire.

This formulation and expression of needs occur in the context of the person's interactional position. As the underlying emotion is engaged with and expanded, the position organized by the emotion also evolves and changes. So, for example, statements made in Step 5 that might be summarized as; "I feel small and inept with you and live in fear of you really seeing this and leaving me, so I go numb and placate," evolve in Step 7 into, "I am tired of numbing out. I want to feel special to you. I want you to hold off on the criticism and quit threatening to leave. I'm not going to feel small in this relationship anymore." This partner now speaks from a position of increased efficacy, where he defines the relationship for himself, rather than reacting to the other's definitions. He is more engaged with his own emotional experience and speaks from an accessible rather than distant and inaccessible position. When his partner is able to join him here, not only do new bonding events occur, but the relationship also becomes redefined as a secure base. This redefinition then fosters the processes of Step 8, *Problem Solving*, and Step 9, the *Consolidation of New Positions*, and more flexible interaction patterns.

As each partner goes through Step 7 in turn, they are able to stay engaged with their emotional experience and clearly state what it is they need in order to feel safe and connected in the relationship. The attachment needs elaborated in previous steps are now clear and can be expressed directly with a sense of legitimacy. The requests made are about key attachment needs for contact comfort and about responses from the other that are crucial to each person's sense of safety and positive sense of self, rather than about instrumental roles or less emotionally central aspects of the relationship.

This kind of expression constitutes a new interactional stance on the part of the speaker that is more equal and more affiliative. These requests have the quality of a new and authentic attempt at engagement with the other partner, rather than a negotiation or proposed exchange of resources. The word "ask" is also important here. The requests are not expressed as demands on the other, nor are they stated in the context of blaming the other.

At this point, the person is also able to hold this position in a flexible manner, rather than being defensively organized and constricted in his/her responses, perhaps because this new position arises out of an integration of emotional experience, as well as out of a refined sense of how personal emotional experience and interactions with the partner are interconnected. When the other partner makes an accusation, for example, this person is usually able to hold his/her position and admit responsibility, without withdrawing and evoking the negative cycle. A husband might say, "Yes, I did what I have done before. I'm so used to reacting that way. But I don't want you to decide now that I'm not trying and get so mad that I can't get anywhere near you. I'm going to work on me and us so that doesn't happen, and I want you to believe me."

The flowering of the Step 5 process is seen here in the way that the person enacts an expanded sense of self, a more differentiated working model of self and other. For example, he/she begins from a position in Steps 1 and 2 of viewing the self as inadequate or unacceptable and the other as critical and dangerous but comes to a position where frailties are viewed as part of being human, and the self is worthy of care and has legitimate needs for such care. He/she is now willing to ask the other to meet those needs, as in, "I am timid. But I can be strong, too. You are not strong all the time, either. It's hard to deal with my fears and find my strength when you're yelling about how wimpy I am. And I want you to stop it. I want some respect. It's hard for piglet and superwoman to be close."

In Step 7, partners are able to present their specific requests in a manner that pulls the spouse toward them and maximizes the possibility that this spouse will be able to respond. The attachment signals are clear (Kobak, Ruckdeschel, & Hazan, 1994) . The nature of the requests made tends to confirm the other spouse's sense of being irreplaceable to the partner and having a powerful effect on him/her. In attachment terms, this is very confirming and compelling. At this point, the spouse may make statement such as, "I never knew that I was that important to you, that you needed me so much." These requests, in fact, address the deprivation and attachment needs of this listening spouse and make it easier for him/her to respond. Blocks to such responsiveness have also been addressed in the process of completing Step 6.

The process of Step 7 is essentially one in which the new emotional experience of Step 5, which has been integrated into relationship interactions in Step 6, is now used to restructure the relationship. The new emotional experience of a partner in Step 5 becomes a new interactional event in Step 7 that redefines the control and affiliation in the relationship.

MARKERS

The therapist intervenes when the following occurs:

1. A partner reiterates or further expands the emotional experience encountered in Step 5 but does not symbolize the needs and wants implicit in this experience. The task for the therapist is to help this partner formulate the needs and wants arising out of this experience and to encourage the expression of these formulations to the other partner.

2. A partner spontaneously begins to state needs and wants to the therapist but does not address these to the other partner or else exits from this process of sharing into a less pertinent, more unfocused dialogue. The task for the therapist is to redirect the process of sharing toward the other partner, or back to a more pertinent focus, and support this person in sharing his/her desires with the other spouse.

3. The other partner either responds openly to the new behavior of the experiencing partner or begins to discount this new behavior. In both cases, the therapist invites the experiencing spouse to continue to respond in an emotionally engaged manner and to state his/her own needs and preferences. The therapist may also need to reflect and validate the difficulties the other observing spouse is having in responding to the changes in his/her partner and in the interaction. On the other hand, if the other partner responds positively, the therapist acknowledges, heightens, and fosters this response.

INTERVENTIONS

As clients enter Step 7, they begin to take more and more initiative and the therapist begins to hand the process over to them, becoming less active but encouraging and redirecting when necessary. The main task is to restructure interactions by tracking and heightening interactions, reframing interactions, and especially fostering the creation of new interactions based on new emotional experience. Some of these new interactions will become new bonding events. More intraphysic interventions, such as evocative responding and empathic conjecture, are used when blocks appear or when people cannot move forward in the process. For example, when a partner suddenly finds it too difficult to ask for the response he/she needs, the therapist may help this person explore this difficulty.

Evocative Responding: Reflections and Questions

The therapist focuses upon the client's emerging experience to help clarify wishes and longings, or to clarify difficulties with expressing such things to the partner.

EXAMPLE

1. **Therapist:** So, if I hear you correctly, you seem to be saying (*summarizes*) that the dread you have of her leaving,

and her threats to do just that, leave you hanging, never on firm ground here, and that makes it difficult to let go and put yourself into the relationship, is that it?

Tim: Yes, and then I close down, but it's not what I want to do. *(He cups one hand in the other and holds them in front of him.)*

Therapist: What you want is? *(Tim does not respond, looking at his hands.)* Your hands are holding each other, like a little nest, a little basket. What is happening right now?

Tim: I don't get to hold her like that. Her investment is mostly back home with her parents, if you see what I mean.

Therapist: Yes. And what you want is?

Tim: I want to hold her.

Therapist: Keep her safe.

Tim: Yes. I want her to put all her eggs in one basket, our basket, to stop running home.

Therapist: To risk leaning on you. *(He nods.)* Can you tell her that please?

EXAMPLE

2. **Therapist:** It's too difficult for you to tell him about this?

   Jane: I don't think I can. It's like, there's no point. He won't hear it *(tears)*.

   Therapist: How are you feeling as you say that Jane?

   Jane: I know what's going to happen. He'll get mad or make excuses.

   Therapist: So it's like, you don't want to risk it.

Empathic Conjecture

It is sometimes necessary to help clients symbolize their longings, which they have often pushed aside to maintain the stability of the relationship and to lessen their own sense of deprivation.

EXAMPLE

Marion: This relationship has been so hard. I think I've buried any hope very deep.

Therapist: You're not sure you want to hope again?

Marion: Right. Sometimes it's okay to just go through the motions, live as chums.

Therapist: It's like all the longings, all the dreams you had when you first met Harry, are locked away now?

Marion: I guess. (*Cries, then stops, pulls her head up and flips her hair back with her hand. Her face becomes tight.*)

Therapist: Help me understand? It almost feels like, "I won't long again, I won't dream and be disappointed?"

Marion: Exactly. (*She cries again.*)

Therapist: But the tears, . . . what are the tears for Marion? What did you want so much and have to give up?

Marion: (*bursting out*) I wanted to be held, I wanted to be precious, just for a while, just to him. (*Cries quietly.*)

Therapist: And I guess some part of you still wants that? Yes? (*She nods.*)

Tracking and Reflecting the Cycle

At this point in therapy, tracking and reflecting the cycle does not usually involve the negative cycle the couple came in with. It is more likely to involve reflecting changes to the negative cycle and the beginnings of a new, more positive cycle. More specifically, it often involves the tracking and reflection of minisequences that occur as inner and outer realities reflect and create each other. For example, in the session described above, the therapist might reflect and describe the process captured here, in terms of how the wife allowed herself to express her longing, but felt very apprehensive, and so at the last minute she qualified her statement, making it much more ambiguous, and therefore more difficult to respond to. The husband, also playing it safe, then responded only minimally. In reflecting this interaction, the therapist fosters an exploration of the process in which the wife's fears influenced her presentation of needs. This presentation then in turn influenced the husband's responses. The therapist can also replay the process to focus on and to explore a particular part of it.

The therapist also tracks and summarizes any new interactions that occur in Step 7. He/she highlights the risks taken by the experiencing spouse, the responses made by the other, and the attachment possibilities that such interactions hold.

EXAMPLE

Therapist: That's incredible Terry, what you did just then. It takes a lot of courage to do that, to say to June, "Just quit telling me how to place my feet every minute and maybe we can dance together. I'd like to tango with you. If you'd just trust me a little, maybe I can figure out how to dance." And then, June, you said something like, "Well, maybe you can" and laughed. That is pretty different from the first few sessions where the idea of trusting Terry to create this relationship was . . . (*pause*).

June: Intolerable. (*Therapist nods.*) Now I guess I have the sense that he does want to dance.

Therapist: Ah-ha, that makes all the difference. You are both finding new ways to be together, to build a relationship together, yes?

Reframing

The difficulties that partners experience in stating their needs are placed in the frame of their experience of the negative cycle and the expectations and vulnerabilities that arise as a result of that cycle.

EXAMPLE

Therapist: I understand that for you it's like a death-defying risk to ask Steve this, after such a long time of feeling that you were not important to him. (*She nods.*) It must be very scary (*She nods.*) He might . . . ?

June: He might give me all the rational reasons why what I need is inappropriate, and then he'd turn away so that I feel small as well as alone. This is risky.

Therapist: To dare to ask for what you want in the face of such hurt and fear, to hope that he will respond, yes? (*She nods.*)

Restructuring Interactions

The most common intervention at this point in therapy, and sometimes the only intervention necessary is the choreographing of a request and the heightening of a positive response.

EXAMPLE

Therapist: So can you ask her, please, "I want you to start to get out of your tank. I want to be close."

Steve: Yes, I want that, and I'm not going anywhere. I want to be beside you, not in the next yard. I want some tenderness, and I want to give it back.

Therapist: How does it feel to say that, Steve?

Steve: It feels good, like it's real, and I feel taller for saying it. (*Therapist nods and smiles.*)

Therapist: What is it like for you to hear that, Gail?

Gail: It's a bit scary, but well, I think I like it, and (*to her partner*) I really like that you wanted to say it enough to risk it; it's different. It's more like when we were first together.

The therapist would then heighten this event and the possibilities it holds for a secure bond between the couple.

Rather than discussing couple process and end state in this chapter, it seems more appropriate to discuss change events, since the structuring of such change events is a crucial part of Steps 5 to 7 for each partner.

CHANGE EVENTS

The completion of Step 7 for a withdrawn partner is synonymous with the change event, *withdrawer engagement*, and the completion of Step 7 for a critical partner is synonymous with the change event called a *softening*. After they have completed Step 7, both partners are more accessible and responsive and able to communicate directly about their attachment issues, so the therapist can then foster positive bonding events. Once this occurs, the last two steps of therapy, which include the process of termination, can begin.

The two change events mentioned above, withdrawer engagement and softening, have also been described in the original book on EFT (Greenberg & Johnson, 1988), and a transcript of a softening can be found in a book chapter already published (Johnson & Greenberg, 1995). However, the partners' progress through prototypical versions of these events is described here so that the reader can get an idea of the step-by-step process.

Withdrawer Engagement

This shift begins in Step 5, with the owning of emotions underlying the interactional position the person enacts in the relationship, as when:

- A usually withdrawn spouse fully experiences his real fear of contact, with all the weight and dread of his catastrophic expectations, as in, "She'll finally see how pathetic and inadequate I am." (The less engaged partner is often but not always, male).

- He then processes this fear with the therapist, who directs him to share it with his partner. He does so congruently, that is, his verbal and nonverbal messages are clear and consistent. He might say, "I cannot let you see me. Sometimes I feel you must loathe me."

- He then accesses a more specific hurt that he is able to express directly to his spouse, as in, "I am not and can never be your wonderful, exciting first lover. I'm just me, and I can never make it with you. I feel so empty inside." (Part of Step 5).

- His spouse first responds with disbelief and cold detachment, but when validated by the therapist, she begins to struggle with her partner's message as in, "You expect me to believe . . . I hope you do hurt . . . you never told me this . . . I never expected this . . . . It seems so sad . . . . I didn't know I was hurting you . . . . (Part of Step 6).

- Supported by the therapist, the husband stays engaged and focused on his own reactions and the dialogue with his wife. His emotional experience begins to have implications for action, telling him clearly where he is and what he wants. He then feels entitled to his emotions and begins to verbalize these elements, as in, "I can't keep trying to prove I'm worth your caring. I won't spend my life that way, struggling up Everest, dealing with your criticism, and feeling too scared to try and get close. I'd rather sleep by myself and just accept being alone."

- The therapist supports the partner to hear this and helps her deal with her anxiety.

- The therapist encourages the husband to tell his wife his needs and wants. This includes what he can and cannot, will and will not, do in the relationship. He is now actively defining the relationship (the opposite of his previous behavior) as well as himself, his role and desires, in it. He now states, "I want to feel desired, like I just might be someone you like to be with. I don't want to hide. I want you to help me learn about how to be close." (Step 7)

He now appears powerful rather than powerless, engaged with his emotions rather than avoiding them, present in the interaction rather than elusive, and seeking for rather than avoiding connection.

This sequence has been simplified to present clearly how this process evolves. Of course, there are various exits and distractions and points along the way where couples stall or become "stuck." After this change event occurs, there is also an integration of this experience into the person's sense of self and into the relationship. A partner will then come into the session and talk about himself/herself more positively or be able to interact with the partner differently. He/she will also take pragmatic steps to change the structure of the relationship at home, such as making more decisions or being different with the children. He/she is moving into Steps 8 and 9. The pace of the process is unique to each individual. Some partners can complete this process in 5 to 6 sessions, while others need more. The therapist adapts the pace of the process to each person's style.

Softening

This shift begins in Step 5 and is often stimulated by the movement of the other partner to a more accessible position, as in the re-engagement event.

Rather than focusing on the faults of the other, partners now begin to focus more on the self, accessing powerful attachment-related fears and/or experiences, which organize their behavior in relation to their spouse. These fears and experiences are experienced intensely and processed anew in the session, and the relevance for the present interaction is heightened, as in, "I promised myself to never count on anyone again. Men will always betray you. You can't be that vulnerable. You might disintegrate. So I smack first and hold my soft sides in."

As a wife, who is beginning this process, tells her partner this, he is able to be more responsive than he was previously. This often enables her to continue to process her inner experience and/or it allows the therapist to really focus on her immediate and clear reluctance to engage the other spouse. The wife, in this example, may access considerable grief, as she allows herself to touch the longing for, and the felt dangers of, connection with the other. Specific experiences in this and in other relationships, as well as specific hurts and key incidents, are accessed and reprocessed, as in, "I have barbed wire around me, so he can't get in. I see the image of him smiling at another woman and turning his back on me, and I go cold, cold." (Step 5) The therapist then helps her share her experience with her spouse, as in, "I can't let you in," and helps the spouse respond in a caring manner. (Step 6)

This partner's definitions of self and other become clear as she expands and intensifies her engagement in her experience of connection and disconnection. The therapist helps her to explore these definitions and to engage emotionally with her partner whenever she can, as in, "The panic I feel when he blocks me off like that; I can't stand it. It's like a soft glove around my throat, suffocating me. I feel so naked, so helpless. I will do anything not to feel that." The therapist asks her to tell her partner about the panic, or perhaps to tell him, "I won't let you do this to me." (Step 5)

This partner's needs and longing now come to the fore, and the therapist helps her formulate them and share them with her partner, as, "I want you to hold me, to help me feel safe. I need you to help me hold back the dark." (Step 7)

As this partner addresses her attachment needs with her partner from a softer, more vulnerable stance, the contact between them is intense and authentic. At this point, the therapist attempts to be as unobtrusive as possible and to support the couple as they take their first turn at a new dance of reaching, allowing themselves to be moved, and coming together in the beginnings of trust. As mentioned previously, a transcript of a softening event can be found elsewhere (Johnson & Greenberg, 1995).

How quickly this takes hold outside of the session and is integrated into the relationship depends on the individual couple. This is also the work of the last two steps of therapy.

8

A SECURE BASE: EFT STEPS 8 AND 9

"She's way more available. She holds my hand in bed."

"We fight but she's not a stranger, and she's not the enemy."

"I can say when I'm insecure and that changes everything."

This chapter describes the termination phase of EFT, Step 8, facilitating the emergence of new solutions to old issues and problems, and Step 9, consolidating the new positions the partners take with each other. These new positions are more flexible and foster accessibility and responsiveness. The relationship now becomes *a secure base* from which to explore the world and deal with the problems it presents and a *safe haven* that provides shelter and protection.

STEP 8

The change events that have occurred in the previous steps now have a direct impact on the couple's ability to problem solve and cooperate as partners in their everyday life.

How does this impact occur? First, pragmatic instrumental concerns are no longer arenas for the couple's emotional struggles. *Issues become much simpler when they do not evoke attachment insecurities, power struggles, and battles over self and relationship definition.* For example, the problem of the family finances remains just that, rather than becoming the trigger for the negative interactional cycle, where one spouse blames and criticizes the other, and the other gives up and refuses to talk. The process becomes one of addressing a common problem rather than conducting a negotiation with the enemy.

Second, the atmosphere of safety and trust that has begun to develop fosters the exploration of issues, as well as the ability of each partner to stay engaged in the process of discussion. Third, the couple spends less time and energy regulating their negative emotions and protecting their individual vulnerabilities. The partners then tend to use the problem-solving skills they have more effectively. Fourth, and perhaps most importantly, the nature and meaning of the problems that the partners face change as a result of the change in the relationship context. Long hours at the office no longer mean that the husband is having an affair with his work; they mean that he has a demanding job. The partners define their relationship problems differently and face them together, as a unit, rather than alone, as isolated individuals.

Research on EFT found that adding the teaching of communication/problem-solving skills did not improve EFT's effectiveness (James, 1991). In fact couples seem to be able to solve problems better after EFT, despite the fact that they have received no formal teaching in this area in therapy (Johnson & Greenberg, 1985). This is not surprising in the context of the EFT model, which does not see such a lack of skill as crucial in the etiology and/or maintenance of marital distress. However, it is true that, as in all therapies, the couple learns new behaviors, even if they are not directly taught.

In EFT, the therapist models new ways to speak to and reach each partner, simply by engaging in this process while the other observes. The process of therapy also shows, in a dramatic and alive manner, what partners can do and who they can be when they feel safe and their experience is validated. The therapist also responds to each partner in terms of his/her attachment insecurities and so models this perspective for the other partner.

The process of addressing pragmatic issues more effectively often begins when the withdrawn partner reengages and begins to take initiative in redefining the relationship. A husband suggests, for example, that the chaotic state of the basement is no longer a problem since he is now clear and able to assert that he is not willing to clean it. And since he understands that the cluttered basement is a long-standing source of frustration for his wife, he has just taken the initiative and hired someone to take care of it. However, larger, more significant issues are usually not resolved until both partners have gone through Step 7. Some issues may also involve life dilemmas that cannot be resolved in any absolute sense but perhaps can be managed more effectively, such as the problem of caring for a chronically ill child or the problem of a career that makes difficult demands, such as frequent postings to new cities or countries.

Markers: Step 8

In Step 8, the therapist intervenes when:

- In the later part of the process of re-engagement, a partner begins to own his/her part in, or perspective on, the pragmatic issues in the relationship. This perspective is now more proactive and opens up new possibilities for problem solving. For example, a husband states that he understands his wife's concerns over finances and is ready to take care of this, so he has arranged to deposit an amount of money each month in the family account. He then intends to run his business on his own terms, without his wife's interference. The task for the therapist is to support the re-engaging partner's initiative, while helping the other spouse to be open to and to respond to such actions. The therapist also helps the couple to articulate the effect this problem-solving process has on the relationship and on the pattern of the couple's interactions.

• When both partners have completed Step 7, the couple
  begins to discuss long-standing life dilemmas facing
  them and/or decisions that in the past have been a source
  of alienation (such as whether to have another child).
  Such issues have not been resolved due to the conflict
  in the relationship and also because the significance of
  certain issues is often intricately tied to the way in which
  the relationship is defined. For example, how much
  money to invest in a cottage may well be a very minor
  problem by the end of therapy, despite the fact that it
  has fueled many long arguments over the years. This is
  because the cottage no longer represents a valued refuge
  from the marriage for the wife or a symbol of imminent
  separation for her husband. The task for the therapist is
  to facilitate discussion and exploration while allowing
  the couple to find their own solutions. The therapist's
  focus is on how the dialogue about such issues can be a
  source of intimacy and contact, as well as on how to help
  the couple confront obstacles to positive responding.

STEP 9

Step 9 concerns the consolidation of the new, more responsive
positions both partners now take in the interaction and the
integration of the changes made in therapy into the everyday
life of the relationship and into each person's sense of self. In
general, the therapist's main goal here is to identify and support healthy, constructive patterns of interaction. The therapist's concern is also to help the couple to construct an
overview of the therapy process and to appreciate the changes
they have made. The therapist helps the couple construct a
coherent and satisfying narrative that captures their experience of the therapy process and their new understanding of
the relationship.

This narrative or story can be used to validate and encourage
the couple and can act as a positive reference point for the
future. The story contains the differentiation of past ways of

interacting and their emotional underpinnings, as well as the shift to current ways of interacting and how the couple journeyed from one to the other. In particular, the story focuses upon the ways they have found to exit from the negative cycle and create positive interactions. The therapist highlights the couple's courage, as well as the various times when they both took risks and made changes. The therapist also highlights the potential of the relationship to protect and nurture them in the future. At this stage in therapy, the therapist follows more than leads, commenting on the couple's process rather than directing it as in earlier stages of therapy. The couple is encouraged to articulate future dreams and goals for the relationship.

When both partners have reached Step 9, termination issues are also addressed. Such issues usually include the expression of fears as to what will happen to the relationship without the therapy sessions, the discussion of the likelihood of relapse into the old cycle and how the couple will deal with that, and questions about how the process of marital distress or improvement evolved. The couple is encouraged to turn to each other, rather than to the therapist, for support around these issues. Original issues also come up again here for review and emotional closure. The goal is for the couple to leave therapy not only non-distressed, but also able to maintain an emotional engagement that will allow them to continue to strengthen the bond between them. This then creates a secure base where each partner can continue to develop his/her sense of self and efficacy in the world.

Markers: Step 9

The therapist intervenes when:

- The couple are able, in the session, to enact new positions and new positive cycles, as well as to relate incidents of such cycles occurring outside of therapy. The contact between the couple is now obviously and tangibly different from the negative interactional pattern seen in the first sessions. The task for the therapist is to high-light these changes and to relate them to the security of the relationship, it's future health, and the expanded sense of self of each of the partners. By symbolizing and heightening the changes the couple have made, the therapist helps the couple formulate these changes in palpable and concrete terms, thus enabling the couple to integrate them into their view of the relationship.

- The couple suggests that they do not need the therapist anymore and are able to be specific about the changes they have each made, as well as how these changes have affected their relationship. They also express fears about not having the "safety net" of the therapy sessions. The task is to validate the couple's strengths and ability to sculpt their relationship to fit their evolving needs, as well as to reassure them and leave them equipped to deal with any reoccurrence of the negative cycle. The therapist also fosters their commitment to maintaining emotional engagement and a positive bond.

The therapist stresses that the changes that have been made belong to the couple and actively discourages the attribution of changes to his/her knowledge and/or skill. The possibility of booster sessions in the future is sometimes left open but framed as probably being unnecessary. When necessary, such sessions usually consist of two or three sessions after a particular crisis occurs, for example, when the death of a child or an illness in one of the partners severely impacts the relationship.

INTERVENTIONS, STEPS 8 AND 9

The therapist reflects the process of interaction between the couple and validates the new emotions and responses they share and enact. This is usually done with less therapist direction and with less intensity than in previous sessions. The therapist becomes most active when this process begins to be derailed by a response from one of the partners. The therapist uses evocative responding to process this partner's experience and to diffuse blocks to positive responding. Empathic conjecture is, at this point in therapy, largely unnecessary. If heightening occurs, it is the specific changes made by the couple that are heightened. The restructuring of the couple's interaction that has occurred in therapy is made explicit by crystallizing present positions and cycles, by comparing them directly to the initial positions and cycles, and by heightening specific new responses. Throughout the final sessions, the therapist comments on the process from the metaperspective of attachment and the attachment process. Some examples of interventions follow:

Reflection and Validation of New Patterns and Responses

EXAMPLE

Therapist: I noticed there, Mike, that you were able to identify your impulse to run and hide, but then you just kept right on sharing and reaching for Mary. Do you know what I mean?

Mike: Yes, I can do that now but not all the time. It's 'cause she doesn't seem so dangerous anymore, and maybe I feel stronger?

Therapist: Yes, it takes a lot of strength to do that, and it helped Mary stay with you and not get angry. Is that right, Mary?

Evocative Responding

EXAMPLE

Therapist: Can I just stop you for a minute, Jim. Things seemed to be going pretty well there for a moment, (*Jim nods*) but then something happened that changed the dance. Do you know what I mean?

Jim: Yes, she used that word "needy" and I freaked. That used to be a big put down between us; she'd call me needy, and I'd feel like I was some kind of defective idiot. That word is pretty loaded for me, so I got aggressive, like she was still the enemy.

Therapist: Can you tell her about that feeling of being defective, Jim, and how it affects you and your ability to keep talking? Can you help her understand . . . ?

The therapist here redirects the interaction back toward a dialogue that is potentially intimate and constructive.

Reframing

The therapist frames new responses as alternatives to the old cycle and places old and new cycles in the context of intimate attachment. The therapist provides the frame for the couple's construction of the narrative "the way we used to be" and "the way we are now and can be in the future." The therapist, for example, may talk about how each partner now helps the other behave in a responsive and accessible manner and actively helps create attachment security for the other.

EXAMPLE

Therapist: So, when David does this, tells you his fears, you feel really important to him and really connected. And that helps you stay out of the depression and stay more involved in the relationship, yes?

Restructuring Interactions

The therapist now consolidates the new positions the partners take with each other, by focusing and commenting explicitly on the nature of these responses. In a sense, the therapist summarizes the restructuring that has already occurred in previous sessions or encourages the couple to create their own summary. The therapist also occasionally choreographs interactions that solidify new responses.

EXAMPLE

Therapist: You know, it really hit me just now, Carey, when you were discussing the incident at the party, how different you are with each other, compared to a few months ago.

Carey: (*laughs*) A few months ago that would have been the start of World War III. And we can still have those conflagrations.

Therapist: Aha, those fights still happen sometimes, kind of like a relapse.

Carey: But we can get out of them now and talk about them.

Therapist: How are you different, Carey? What has changed for you?

Carey: Well, my whole focus was to never let her get to me, you know, to numb out if I had to, and that would just fuel her rage.

COUPLE PROCESS AND END STATE

What do the couple look like at the end of therapy? At this point, when the therapist watches the interaction, it is difficult, or impossible, to identify fixed rigid positions. Both partners might withdraw for a moment. Both can get angry and critical. But both take risks in the relationship, and both are able to reveal their own vulnerabilities and respond to their partners in a caring way. In short, *negative interactions are more fluid and are processed differently, and they also have less impact on the way the relationship is defined.* On the other hand, positive interactions are more apparent and are also acknowledged and owned. The quality of the contact between partners has shifted towards safety, closeness, and trust. The way the partners talk about each other, the attributions they make, have taken on a more positive and compassionate

tone, and in general, the way the couple talk to each other
has changed.

The quality of the interaction is perhaps best captured by
the contrast between a dialogue where each person defends
against the other and is concerned with regulating his/her own
negative affect, and a dialogue where each partner is actively
discovering the other, as well as the self in relation to the
other. Attachment theory suggests that in young children exploration behaviors are fostered by a sense of safety and security; in adults, too, a sense of security seems to foster the
curiosity and openness essential to adult intimacy.

Marital therapy does not always result in the creation of a
more connected and intimate relationship. Occasionally, the
process of clarifying the cycles of interaction and the underlying emotions results in the couple deciding to separate or to
live together in a parallel and relatively separate fashion. Then
the picture at the end of therapy looks a little different. The
negative cycle has been modified, and the couple are no longer
blaming each other or becoming stuck in painful impasses,
where one tries to please while the other keeps his/her distance. In these cases, however, the positive cycles are much
more constricted and result in calm, effective negotiations,
rather than intimate contact. For example, the couple may
agree that they do not fit as spouses, but they have given each
other much and wish to stay together for another three years
to bring closure to their task as parents. They are clear that at
that time they will both be free to pursue their own goals and
other relationships.

If termination evokes great anxiety in one or both of the
partners, the therapist uses evocative responding to help such
partners explore their fears and directs them to discuss these
fears with each other and ask for each other's help in dealing
with them on a day-to-day basis. Generally, if the process of
therapy has gone well, the partners face the end of the sessions
with a certain trepidation, but they also feel more in control
of their relationship than ever before. They are ready to leave
the safe base of therapy and fly on their own.

The process of marital therapy may be relatively more intense and all-encompassing for some partners than for others. As people struggle with defining their intimate relationship, they also inevitably struggle with defining themselves and sometimes events evolve into an existential crisis for one of the partners. The term existential crisis is used here as described in Yalom's (1980) text on existential psychotherapy. Sometimes, such partners are already in individual therapy and the marital therapist can confer with the individual therapist to dovetail the two therapy processes. Sometimes, the individual accesses real dilemmas and vivid choice points in the process of marital therapy, that eluded him/her in individual therapy. This process may be contained within the usual framework of EFT, or it may require a few individual sessions at some time in the process. In these cases, the end of therapy is usually more poignant or dramatic, since it involves not only the redefinition of the relationship, but also closure on an existential dilemma. For example, a 50-year-old man who has never been able to commit himself to a relationship, even with his children, struggles in therapy with all the very good reasons he has for his strict boundaries concerning close relationships and his fears concerning closeness. Marital therapy here involved a recognition of his longings for closeness and his fears of depending on another. The end of therapy also involved, then, a resolution of this individual lifelong issue.

To summarize, at the end of therapy the following changes are usually apparent.

Emotional

Negative affect has lessened and is processed and regulated differently. The couple can stay emotionally engaged and can use the relationship to regulate negative affect such as fears and insecurities. Positive affect has been evoked by more positive cycles of interaction. The partners are more engaged with their own emotional experience; they accept their own emotions more, and they can express these emotions in a way that helps their spouse respond to them.

Behavioral

The couple behave differently toward each other, being more accessible and responsive in the session and in their daily lives. As a result, each one experiences the relationship as more supportive. Behavior in interactions is generally less constricted and more responsive to the other's communications. Specific attachment behaviors change. For example, partners now ask for what they need, and they can ask in a way that helps their partner respond. Other behaviors not explicitly addressed in therapy also change, such as the amount and quality of the couple's sexual contact and their ability to problem solve.

Cognitive

The partners perceive each other differently. They have had a new experience of the other in the sessions, and so they make different and more positive attributions about the other's responses. They have also included new elements in their definitions of the other partner and of themselves; in attachment terms, their specific models of the other, and of self in relation to the other, have been modified. They also have a different metaframework for relationships in general, since they have experienced their relationship through the therapist's attachment perspective.

Interpersonal

Negative cycles are contained, and new positive cycles are enacted. The partners are now able to "unlatch" (Gottman, 1979) from self-reinforcing negative interactions, as well as to initiate new responses that evoke more positive responses from the spouse and create more overall emotional engagement.

9

BUMPS ON THE PATH: CLINICAL QUESTIONS AND ANSWERS

In this chapter, clinical issues and questions that arise during the EFT training process are discussed. The kinds of issues addressed in this chapter are prognostic indicators for EFT, dealing with impasses in therapy and integrating EFT with other approaches.

QUESTION: WHAT TYPES OF COUPLES AND/OR INDIVIDUALS IS EFT PARTICULARLY SUITED FOR AND, CONVERSELY, NOT SUITED FOR?

In general, EFT works best for couples who still have some emotional investment in their relationship and some willingness to learn about how they may have each contributed to the problems in the relationship. This is probably true for all kinds of marital therapy. Being motivated to change, being willing to look at one's own behavior, and being willing to engage in the process of therapy, including taking emotional risks, are factors that have been generally associated with change in psychotherapy.

There is also some research (Johnson & Talitman, in press) that allows for more specific predictions as to who will benefit from EFT. This research found that EFT worked best when the couple's alliance with the therapist was high. Presumably, this is because the alliance enabled couples to participate fully and engage in the process of therapy. The quality of this alliance was a much more powerful and general predictor of treatment success than the initial distress level. What mattered most was the bond with the therapist, the sense of shared goals, and, in particular, the perceived relevance of the tasks presented by the therapist, rather than how distressed the partners were at the beginning of therapy. This perception of the relevance of the tasks that couples are asked to engage in could be a reflection of the skill of the therapist who is able to tailor these tasks to each couple and to frame them in a way that is meaningful for them. It could also be a reflection of the general nature of EFT, that is, EFT may be particularly suited to couples who are lacking in intimacy and emotional connection and who see a focus on the quality of their attachment as relevant to their problems.

The central concern for the EFT therapist then, particularly in the initial stages of therapy, must be to make a strong positive connection with each partner; to create a secure base from which each partner can explore the relationship. Stated differently, the central issue becomes whether or not a couple can engage in therapy and how accessible they are to the therapist, rather than how great or intractable their problems appear to be.

Does engagement in EFT require that partners be particularly expressive or aware of their emotions? The research referred to above (Johnson & Talitman, in press) found that a lack of expressiveness or a reluctance to self-disclose did not hamper progress in EFT. In fact, EFT seemed to be particularly powerful with male partners who were described by their wives as inexpressive. This may be because when such partners do express themselves in the supportive environment of EFT, the results are often very compelling for themselves and for their partners. This research also provided evidence that men who are older (over 35) seem to be more responsive to

EFT, perhaps because men tend to see issues of intimacy and attachment as more relevant as they get older.

For female partners, the variable that had the most impact on treatment success was the amount of faith they had that their spouse still cared for them. This was a powerful predictor of both partners' adjustment and intimacy at treatment termination and follow-up. In a culture where women have traditionally taken most of the responsibility for maintaining close bonds, this may represent some kind of bottom line, which can be expressed as: If the female partner still has some willingness to risk with and trust in the other spouse, then marital therapy, at least this kind of marital therapy, has more chance of success. Conversely, if the female partner is unwilling to risk herself and engage emotionally with her partner, even in a supportive environment, then the possibilities for the relationship may be limited.

This is, then, a crucial variable for the EFT therapist to attend to throughout therapy. A severe lack of trust would seem to be an insurmountable obstacle to emotional engagement and to marital happiness in general. Indeed, evidence is accumulating that *emotional disengagement*, rather than other elements, such as the inability to resolve disagreements, is predictive of long-term unhappiness and instability in marriage (Gottman, 1994), and is also associated with a lack of success in various forms of marital therapy (Jacobson & Addis, 1993). Disengagement is associated with a lack of sexual contact, affection, and tenderness. It can be seen as an extremely insecure or damaged emotional bond, where emotional connection is experienced as too dangerous to be tolerated or is no longer desired. In the latter case, such disengagement may signal the end of the process of separation distress as identified by Bowlby (1969), which involves protest, clinging, and depression and the beginning of detachment and dissolution.

The level of traditionality in a couple's marriage does not seem to affect outcome in EFT (Johnson & Talitman, in press). Couples in which a very affiliative woman is married to an independence-oriented man, who would then most often be expected to display the classic criticize, pursue/stonewall, withdraw pattern identified as so deadly for marital happiness (Gottman, 1991), seem to be able to make progress in EFT. In other marital therapies, this was not found to be the case (Jacobson, Follette, & Pagel, 1986)

Another dimension that intuitively would seem to be important for the EFT therapist is that of rigidity versus flexibility. It is more difficult for the therapist to intervene effectively if a member of the couple has very constricted and rigid ways of processing his/her experience and of interacting with the other. The experience of pain tends to narrow human consciousness (Bruner, 1990), and for all couples part of the EFT process is to expand awareness and experience. However, there are some individuals with very rigidly held views of self and other, as well as very limited ways of regulating affect, for whom the expansion of such views and ways of processing are too high a price to pay for modifying their relationship. *In attachment terms, it is more difficult to intervene when working models are impermeable and thus unresponsive to new experience.* In the EFT process, this can result in either the less engaged partner refusing to become more involved or, more frequently, the more critical partner being unable to complete the softening change event.

EFT has also been used to address a wider spectrum of problems than marital distress, which is sometimes only part of a broader clinical picture. For example, EFT seems to work well with couples where the female partner is clinically depressed, alleviating the depression and the marital distress (Dessaulles, 1991). It can also be used in a shortened form to increase intimacy in mildly distressed or nondistressed spouses (Dandeneau & Johnson, 1994). It appears to be particularly effective with couples experiencing chronic family stress and grief—for example, parents of chronically ill children. In a study with these couples, EFT not only improved marital adjustment, but also individual depression levels and the perceived stress involved in caring for the ill child (Walker, et al., in press). At two-year follow-up, these results remained stable (Walker & Manion, in preparation). In case studies (rather than in empirical research studies), EFT has been successfully implemented as part of the treatment of sexual abuse survivors and in cases where one or both of the partners were suffering from post-traumatic stress disorder (Johnson & Williams-Keeler, 1996).

When is EFT not used? EFT is not used with separating couples, where pragmatic negotiation or individual grief work may be more appropriate, or with abusive couples, where expressions of vulnerability are likely to be dysfunctional and place the abused partner more at risk. Abusive partners are referred to group or individual therapy to help them deal with their anger and control issues. They are offered EFT only after this process is complete and their partners no longer feel at risk. However, in practice the therapist has to sometimes make a judgment as to what is abusive. One abusive incident does not necessarily make an abusive relationship. The most useful guides here are the victim's experience of the abuse and the therapist's own observation of the couple's interaction.

There are relationships in which no physical violence has ever occurred but where verbal abuse in the form of threats, denigrating comments, and deliberate moves to hurt and intimidate the other occur on a frequent basis. The therapist has then to decide whether encouraging the victim of this abuse to move into Step 3, accessing underlying feelings, is functional or even ethical. If the therapist judges that EFT (and perhaps marital therapy in general) is not the best intervention at this point, he/she paints a diagnostic picture of the relationship and the cycles of interaction, before outlining the choices the partners have open to them. To encourage the abusive spouse to go for treatment, the therapist often frames the problem in terms of finding help to stop anger or violence from further taking over and destroying the relationship and the family. This kind of frame is similar to the externalizing interventions described by White and Epston (1990). From a more traditional dynamic point of view, it frames the violence as ego-dysyntonic or foreign to the abusive spouse's nature and well-being; it is then this person's enemy, an enemy that is able to create havoc in his family life and his sense of self-esteem. This frame encourages the abusive partner to tackle the problem.

QUESTION: HOW DOES THE EFT THERAPIST DEAL WITH IMPASSES IN THERAPY?

The general answer to this question is that the therapist reflects the impasse, both in terms of specific interactions and specific emotional responses, and heightens the "stuckness" of the couple. As the couple enacts the impasse again and again, different elements come to the fore, and responses become more and more differentiated. The positions the partners take with each other become more and more vivid and immediate, as do their interactional consequences. As the emotions inherent in these positions become reprocessed, new responses and perceptions begin to emerge. *Movement comes here not as a result of trying to do something different but as a result of experiencing fully what it is that one does when threatened in the relationship, as well as how compelling and legitimate one's responses are.*

This dialogue itself also defines a new kind of contact between the couple, which also opens the door for change. For example, it is more intimate and engaged (and therefore a step out of the impasse) to tell one's spouse that you cannot and will not ask for love because, as you experience it, that is more excruciatingly demeaning, than it is to blame, justify your anger, and withdraw from the dialogue. At the very least, the therapist creates safety, maintains the focus of the session, and then simply blocks the exits the partners usually take, so that the impasse is confronted. The most common impasse encountered in EFT is when the second partner, usually the critical partner, enters Steps 5 to 7 and the opportunity for reciprocal emotional engagement presents itself. This most often presents as a crisis of trust in that this partner sometimes has great difficulty confronting his/her hopes and fears and putting him/herself in the other person's hands, even though this other person now seems accessible and responsive. Often the therapist does not have to confront the couple concerning an impasse; the process itself confronts them.

Are there different kinds and levels of impasses? It would appear so. In extreme impasses, the couple sometimes may not find a way through but may actually integrate the impasse into their relationship, thus modifying the corrosive power of the problem. For example, one partner, who had been the victim of sexual abuse when young, had very clear limits and requirements around sex and physical affection. As a result of therapy, the husband was able to accept his wife's limits. The problem behavior remained but did not now have the dire consequences it once had for the relationship. The husband's willingness to accept certain limits in the sexual area also strengthened the bond and increased the level of intimacy between the couple. This was possible largely because, by the end of therapy, these limits did not threaten the attachment bond between the partners.

In other extreme impasses, one partner may decide that he/she cannot do anything that makes a difference and also cannot live in the relationship as it is. The couple may then decide to separate, or they will stay together with very modified expectations of the relationship. In such cases, the therapist presents diagnostic pictures of the impasse and outlines the choices open to the couple.

One kind of impasse that presents itself in EFT can be labeled the attachment "crime" or "trauma." This is a critical incident that captures the essence of, or symbolizes, the attachment betrayal or disappointment that has occurred in the relationship and is accessed every time movement toward more contact occurs. The disappointed partner uses this incident as a reference point for all the negative experience in the present relationship, while the other partner is continually frustrated and alienated by the reiteration of the incident. Such incidents are not "in the past," but are an alive and current part of the relationship. The EFT therapist helps the couple process this incident as it arises in the session and reprocess the emotions inherent in the event. The attachment fears and losses associated with this critical incident or "crime" have often not been previously expressed or even clearly formulated. What is expressed is usually blame and criticism of the other partner.

Some attachment traumas from the individual person's past, such as childhood sexual abuse, may require individual therapy in addition to marital therapy. Often, however, the trauma occurred in the present relationship, and even if it evokes similar childhood experiences, it can be worked within this context. The EFT therapist supports both partners—the one in exploring the experience of the trauma further and allowing the consequences for present interactions to emerge and the other in being able to listen and acknowledge this person's experience.

For example, a wife who reiterates an incident in which, as she perceived it, her husband sided with an employer against her by agreeing that she was incompetent and should resign, is encouraged to expand this experience in the session. She accesses grief, a sense of helpless isolation, and fears about how deserving she is of his love. The husband is then able to respond to expressions of these feelings and begins to acknowledge that this experience has made it difficult for his wife to share herself with him. This is already a shift from the usual impasse for this couple, where no matter how he approached her, she attacked him and refused to engage with him emotionally.

QUESTION: HOW DOES THE EFT THERAPIST DEAL WITH PAST EXPERIENCES?

EFT does deal with past experiences insomuch as they are enacted in present interactions. Intense affect, as it arises in present interactions, evokes past experiences that help the person construe, or make sense of, the present situation. In attachment terms, intense negative affect may call up old unresolved attachment hurts and losses and the working models that are associated with these experiences. The person moves from the present experience, "You betrayed me. I knew I couldn't trust you," to "I have never been able to trust anyone." The grief and pain of past hurts then infuse the present situation and help to determine how the person will regulate this affect, as in, "So I will shut you out and shut my longings down, like

I did before." Past unresolved hurts and working models of attachment thus become part of the present; they are alive and accessible in the session. The EFT therapist will evocatively respond to such experience, helping the person reprocess such emotions and/or helping the spouse respond appropriately.

The EFT therapist also helps each partner construct a brief focused narrative of his/her attachment history, as it pertains to perceptions and responses in the present relationship. This helps to validate the way a particular partner experiences the present relationship, and it also helps the other partner to see this person in a wider context. Indeed, in EFT, past experiences are referred to in order to validate and legitimize present responses, particularly ways of dealing with attachment needs and associated emotions. For example, the therapist might validate a partner's fear of trusting her spouse in the light of the abandonment she experienced with her parents when her baby brother was born. This may also help her partner to see her withdrawal at certain times in the interaction in a more compassionate light.

In EFT, however, *the arena of change is the present relationship.* The client is not taken back to the past to gain insight and resolve past hurts; rather, the echoes of the past are dealt with where they are lived, in the present. If the present relationship can be made more whole and secure, the past has been changed in that its ramifications have been modified. The past, in the form of personal sensitivities, is then integrated in a new way into the present. In addition, new experiences in the present challenge partners' working models, which are reflections of past experience, thus creating new expectations and new ways of regulating affect. Through the clearer, more coherent, and more complete processing of present attachment experiences, both the past and the present are then reorganized.

QUESTION: DOES THE EFT THERAPIST EVER LIMIT EMOTION?

Emotion in EFT is experienced rather than discussed. It is felt rather than simply labeled and can be intense and dramatic.

Constriction of emotional experience and expression is also seen as a key part of marital problems. However, ventilation or expression for its own sake is not the goal in EFT. The experience and expression of emotion are powerful, and that power can be both positive and negative. The specter of uncontrolled emotion has been the rationale for individual and marital therapists' keeping the expression of affect under tight control or avoiding it altogether (Mahoney, 1991). In experiential approaches to therapy, emotion has been viewed more positively (Johnson & Greenberg, 1994). Nevertheless, the EFT therapist also modulates the expression and experience of affect. If affect is viewed as the music of the dance, then there are times when the therapist needs to turn the music down or vary the tune, just as there are times when he/she might turn the music up. When and how does the EFT therapist do this?

The therapist moves to contain affect that threatens to overwhelm either of the partners and their ability to stay coherently engaged with their experience or the interaction. In a volatile attack/attack cycle, the therapist will reflect the emotions and the cycle; this tends to slow the cycle down and reduce reactivity. If necessary, the therapist will also actively block, divert, and refocus mutual blaming, as well as evoke softer feelings, perhaps of sadness or hurt.

On an individual level, the therapist will validate and support an individual in the midst of painful emotions. As in other experiential and dynamic therapies, the therapeutic relationship "holds" the client's emotional experience, making it safer for that client to confront that experience. The therapist's comfort and reassurance helps the individual stay engaged with, but not be overwhelmed by, affective experience. The therapist's ability to accurately reflect, accept, and crystallize such experience also helps the person regulate the experience. If appropriate, the therapist will also help the other partner attune to and respond to this person's affect in a manner that renders this affect less burdensome. For example, anger is defused by the other's listening but exacerbated by the other's defensive withdrawal, just as fear is lessened by the other's expressed compassion.

On an interpersonal level, there are times when the therapist may interrupt expressions of negative affect, particularly secondary affect, such as reactive anger at the other partner. The therapist will redirect the process to the other partner's experience or to the underlying experience of the blaming partner. The therapist may also reframe an expression of negative affect so that it can be useful rather than destructive in the therapy process, helping a partner move from "No one could trust you. You are so mean." to " I won't trust you. I'll show you that you can't control me."

The line between containment and the reprocessing of emotion, one of the central tasks in EFT, becomes murky here. There is a sense in which the structured process of EFT, in itself, can be said to modulate and direct and, therefore, to contain emotion. The therapist also interrupts the expression of emotion when such expression is inconsistent with the present focus of the session or seems to be a distraction, an exit, from the exploration of immediate primary feelings. The therapist will reflect the emotion expressed and validate the person's need to be heard on this topic but will redirect the session back to the more pertinent experience.

QUESTION: DO INDIVIDUALS CHANGE IN THE COURSE OF EFT?

In the first book on EFT (Greenberg & Johnson, 1988), there is a section on addressing individual symptomatology, such as depression and phobias (pp. 189-93). Individual symptoms are viewed in that text as reflecting and constructing relationship rules and patterns of interaction. This seems particularly pertinent in relation to individual symptoms such as depression in women, since women tend to define themselves in the context of their interpersonal relationships and tend to be very negatively affected by the symptoms of marital distress, such as the withdrawal of the male partner (Christensen & Heavey 1990; Roberts & Krokoff, 1990). It can be argued that EFT, focusing as it does on emotional connection, may particularly address the needs that are most commonly expressed by women, making EFT a particularly appropriate intervention when the female partner is suffering from such symptoms and also experiencing marital distress.

However, even for partners who have no such symptoms, successful EFT involves an expansion and further differentiation of each partner's sense of self, focusing as it does on basic needs for security and connection, on how these are dealt with, and on how people are defined in interactions with significant others. Certainly, there is evidence that, by the end of therapy, partners perceive each other differently (Greenberg, James, & Conry, 1988), and respond differently to each other; thus, partners get different feedback about who they are and tend to feel more accepted and acceptable. Each partner has also more fully experienced his/her emotional responses and attachment needs and has been encouraged to interact in new ways with the other. The unassertive man has risked being assertive, and the detached woman has risked asking for what she wants. This new experience changes the sense that people have of themselves and their abilities. *Rigid constricted interpersonal cycles narrow down the experience, presentation, and enactment of self. When these cycles are expanded, the sense of self also expands.*

To a marital therapist like myself who was initially trained as an individual therapist, the power of couples' interventions to call forth new aspects of a partner's individual personality is still surprising. It should not be, since the basic traditional underpinning of the whole psychotherapy enterprise is that new and different encounters with significant others, new kinds of relationships, allow people to change and evolve. Traditionally, such relationships were with therapists. In marital therapy, it is the already formed and powerfully significant relationship with the other spouse that can be used to foster individual growth and to heal individual hurts.

In cases where an individual's position is very circumscribed and rigidly held, the marital therapy process may present this individual with a vivid existential crisis. A man who has played the part of a "Don Juan" all his life, for example, came to therapy mostly motivated by guilt and confronted his inability to "let any one in." This man, who had previously been in years of individual therapy and had a long history of brief, idealized relationships, then accessed grief at the constricted relationships he had experienced with his parents, family, and lovers, as well as his enormous fear of placing himself in a position where anyone could abandon him. Past attachment experiences were touched and echoed forward into the therapy sessions. However, it was in enacting his refusal to connect with his present partner that his models of self and other and his attachment fears became accessible and were able to be reviewed and expanded.

In couples therapy, human beings sometimes enact very basic human dilemmas that are difficult to evoke in individual therapy. This man explored all the ways he had of staying on the outside edge of his own emotional life and his relationships. He faced two dragons: the fear of dying alone, of never having connected with another and the fear of being found wanting and, therefore, abandoned. His partner was able, with the therapist's support, to provide a secure base for him in the sessions, and he was able to face his dragons and make new choices. In such cases, couples therapy incorporates individual therapy. Both of the partners in the above case were seen in several individual sessions, and the process of couples therapy naturally potentiated the individual change process.

QUESTION: HOW DOES THE EFT THERAPIST KNOW WHICH EMOTION TO FOCUS ON?

There are a number of answers to this question. To be concise:

1. **It's best to start where people are.** At the beginning of therapy, the therapist focuses on and reflects the emotions, or even the lack of them, that the couple present. These are often secondary reactive responses, but the EFT therapist begins with the emotions that the partners spontaneously express. This is already a new

experience, in that the partners are usually obsessively focused on each other's behavior, blaming or defending, rather than on the emotion itself, such as anger and how they experience it.

2. **The therapist follows the partners.** As the couple feel more secure in the sessions, the therapist follows each partner to the edge of his/her emotional experience and then encourages exploration. He/she also structures interactional tasks that evoke new emotional experience and expression. The therapist focuses on whatever is most poignant for each partner, tracking each person's experience. It is, therefore, the experiencing person who lets the therapist know where to focus.

3. **The therapist follows the maps provided by his/her own emotions and the drama of the client's relationship.** The EFT therapist has different maps that suggest a particular focus at particular times in therapy. In experiential therapies, one map is the therapist's own sense of empathy, which Guerney (1994) describes as a leap of imagination. The therapist allows him/herself to engage in the client's experience, to taste it, and process it further, using his/her own emotional responses and empathy as a guide to the client's experience.

The second map is the drama of the positions that the couple take in the interaction. Each emotion has a "distinctive dramatic plot" (Lazarus & Lazarus, 1994). Emotional realities are often connected with particular positions. Withdrawal, for example is often associated with a sense of intimidation and helplessness, as well as with a sense of inadequacy or shame.

There are predictable common patterns in the way in which emotional experience organizes interactional responses. The therapist uses his/her knowledge of such patterns as clues to the underlying emotional experience of both partners and as a guide to the new experiences that he/she might heighten to help partners change their positions. For example, the therapist senses that a husband fears his wife's rejection and therefore hides but notes that if the husband could ever allow himself to express anger, this would empower him and revolutionize the way he interacts with his wife.

4. **The therapist uses his/her theory of close relationships as a map.** Attachment theory presents a context for the specific experiences of the partners, helping the therapist understand the client's experience at moments when the client may not and giving the therapist a direction to move in. When the therapist cannot follow the client's experience, such a theoretical map helps the therapist to know where to focus. For example, attachment theory suggests that the only way some children have to maintain relationships with unavailable parents is to minimize their awareness of attachment needs and block out any longing for intimate contact. So, when a partner says that he feels "nothing" in the face of very negative or very positive emotional responses presented by his spouse, this map suggests that it is useful to focus on his lack of response and the possible insecurity and inhibited longing that often organizes such a response.

QUESTION: HOW DOES EMOTIONAL EXPERIENCE EVOLVE IN EFT?

Engagement Expands Emotion

Generally, if one accepts that emotions that are threatening tend to be distorted, avoided, minimized, and constricted on both experiential and expressive levels, engagement with and acceptance of one's emotions tend to clarify and expand them. Some emotions, such as fear and shame, seem to be so painful in and of themselves that a person's attention naturally moves to regulate these emotions, to contain the pain, and reorganize the experience, rather than to engage with and process this emotion further. However, this reorganization (such as initial fear experienced and expressed as anger) often has negative side effects, such as further alienating one's partner.

The expansion of such emotion involves keeping the emotion in focus and processing it fully, rather than allowing it to be immediately reorganized in a way that protects the self. The adaptive action tendencies, crucial information about the self, and attachment needs implicit in the emotion are then available and can be used to organize interactional responses. The EFT therapist will move to block the reorganization of hurt into anger and instead will validate the hurt. This hurt can then evolve into a sense of helplessness and need for the other's reassurance and caring.

Another way of viewing this process is that engagement with one's emotions allows the person to experience conflicting emotional responses, such as a yearning for contact and a fear of such contact and to create a more integrated response.

Specific Interactional Tasks Create New Experience and a New Story

The interactional tasks set by the therapist and the new responses made by the spouse also generate new emotional experience. For example, a spouse's offer of comfort and reassurance challenges his/her partner's sense of abandonment and evokes new emotional responses. The therapist helps the couple to construct a coherent unifying narrative of each person's emotional realities and how these realities define interactions. Couples leave therapy with a sense of how their emotional and interactional responses fit together and create their relationship; they feel more able to create new and more positive emotional experience.

Emotional Processing Naturally Evolves and Has Its Own Pathways

In interactions with significant others, the experience of particular emotions seems to evolve naturally and in predictable ways. For example, in situations of insecurity or threat, a universal way of regulating hurt and shame is to "transform" such experience into secondary anger, or righteous rage, usually expressed in the form of blaming the person who has offended us (Wile, 1994; Pierce, 1994). The anger tends to protect the person from the sting of his/her own emotions and from possible anticipated harm from the other. If the primary response, (the hurt underlying the anger) remains unprocessed, anger organizes inner and outer worlds, tending to evoke responses from the other that continue to fuel the angry response. This kind of anger is very different from the primary anger that arises when an intimidated spouse begins to contact his hurt and fear, which naturally evolves into expressed outrage at his partner's perceived lack of respect for him. The EFT therapist follows the natural pathways of such emotional processing. He/she is able to predict how this processing will evolve and how he/she can heighten and use this process to shift interactional positions.

Particular emotions also evolve in particular ways. One particularly problematic emotion is shame. Tears can bring people together, and anger can be an impetus for assertiveness and respect. But shame, by its nature, hides and divides. Shame also appears to be such an aversive experience that it is seldom used to regulate other emotions in the manner described above (Pierce, 1994). Self-disgust, inadequacy, and a sense of worthlessness that create a model of the self as unlovable and undeserving of care make self-disclosure and the communication of needs and desires seem extremely hazardous.

The most common ways of regulating shame seem to be to become angry at others or to generally numb emotion in attachment contexts and withdraw from contact with others. Thus, the most common ways of regulating this painful emotion tend to create interactions that again evoke the emotion itself, such as rejection from others. As shame is experienced and disclosed, sadness and grief naturally accompany it. If the other partner can respond in a reassuring way, the relief and comfort this acceptance provides acts as an antidote to the shame experience.

Fear is perhaps the most pertinent and endemic emotion in distressed marriages. It evokes compelling fight or flight behavior and constricts how partners perceive and interact with each other. Emotion has been described as an alarm system, a compelling automatic response that takes precedence over other responses; fear is perhaps the most obvious example. Various authors have identified the fears that typically arise in attachment relationships, such as fear of being left or abandoned, fear of being rejected or found unlovable, and fear of being controlled and helpless. Fear as a secondary response is, in most cases, amenable to a therapy such as EFT; the therapist provides safety and support, and the partner is able to express anger, assert him/herself, or express sadness. In EFT change events, it is usually fear, or attachment insecurity, that the person struggles with. In softening events, where a person risks reaching for the other and asking for his/her attachment needs to be met, anger or seeming detachment naturally gives way to powerful fears, which are encountered and processed in the session. These fears can then be regulated with the help of the spouse, who provides comfort.

Comment

Before going on to discuss the integration of EFT with other approaches, it is worth noting that there are clinical issues that are hard to address in written form. Learning to do therapy from a book has been compared to learning to sing a tune by looking at grooves in a record. Issues of timing, for example, are particularly difficult to address in this medium. This and other training issues are addressed in the original text on EFT (Greenberg & Johnson, 1988), which contains extensive examples of interventions and therapy sequences, and by transcripts of therapy printed elsewhere (Johnson & Greenberg, 1992; Johnson & Greenberg, 1995). There is also a training videotape of EFT (Johnson, 1993) that shows excerpts from a complete course of EFT, as given to one couple. One of the best ways to learn EFT is to make tapes of one's own therapy sessions and to replay such tapes, noting couple interactions and responses and the interventions made by the therapist. It is also useful to formulate different and improved interventions and hypothesize about what effects these would have on the process of therapy.

QUESTION: CAN EFT BE INTEGRATED WITH OTHER CURRENT APPROACHES?

Since the conception of EFT, other approaches to marital and family therapy have evolved, specifically narrative and solution-focused approaches. Both of these approaches are constructivist, viewing people's lives as shaped by the meaning they ascribe to their experience. In both, therapists take a non-pathologizing, empowering stance toward their clients and take clients' statements at "face value" (O'Hanlon & Wilk, 1987); they believe what clients say, rather than searching for hidden motives. Hence, there are certain commonalities with EFT, especially with regard to these aspects. EFT, and other experiential interventions, are also constructivist, nonpathologizing, and attempt to accept people as they are as a beginning point in therapy. The points of contact between narrative approaches and EFT are clearer, however, and a discussion of these points can perhaps elucidate EFT interventions further, as well as help readers familiar with narrative approaches to orient themselves to EFT interventions.

EFT and Narrative Approaches

Both EFT and narrative approaches view people as being actively involved in meaning making (Bruner, 1990) that is, as constructing their experience and then using the meaning so constructed to orient themselves to the world and act upon it. Both view this construction as arising from, and being, constrained by, the reality of the social context. For both the EFT and the narrative therapist, objective reality is ultimately unknowable and every way of seeing is also a way of not seeing. What you see depends on where you stand in the landscape.

Both EFT, with its roots in humanistic experiential approaches, and narrative approaches tend to view people in therapy as the experts on their own experience. The therapist is concerned with helping people construct that experience in a way that opens up more choices for them. Neither approach sees the therapist as having a privileged access to truth but views the therapist as a guide in the "reauthoring" or, in EFT, reprocessing of life experience. Both approaches promote a therapeutic stance of faith in people's abilities to solve their problems and both tend to minimize the differences between therapists and clients. Problems are seen as arising from a social context that would likely be as problematic for the therapist as it is for his/her client.

Both approaches are sensitive to the use of language to create new meaning, to reframe events, and create a new context. Both tend to see expression as part of the organization of experience rather than simply a product.

In terms of interventions, there are also certain commonalities. As Minuchin and Nichols (1993) point out, all therapists are storytellers. Many different kinds of therapists also stress and use exceptions to problematic events and/or responses (called unique outcomes in narrative approaches) to empower people and increase their sense of efficacy. Many therapists of different persuasions, including EFT therapists, also consciously create reframes to contradict or rename a dominant problematic pattern or "plot." However, the most significant and unique intervention in narrative approaches is that of externalizing the problem, rendering the taken-for-granted reality strange (White, 1993) and separating it from the person who experiences it. There is a significant commonality with EFT here, in that in EFT the negative interactional cycle is externalized, and both partners are framed as co-constructors and victims of this pattern, which has taken over the relationship.

The most common patterns identified in EFT are pursue/ withdraw and attack/defend, although some couples may also display withdraw/withdraw or attack/attack patterns. These patterns have a life of their own and constrict the partner's interactions, precluding positive emotional engagement. In therapy, the partners learn how they help to evoke from each other the responses they find so distressing and so co-construct the pattern of interactions that defines their relationship. The couple can, therefore, close ranks against the pattern that is sabotaging their relationship. The problem is not "him" or "her," but the "dance we do together." The effects of this pattern on each person are elaborated, although this is done in a different manner in EFT and narrative approaches; narrative therapists being generally much more cognitive and discursive. In the beginning of EFT, this focus on the cycle provides a new context that allows the partners to take responsibility for their behavior, step aside from blaming, and begin to focus on how they share a common fate, rather than being stuck in victim and oppressor roles.

At other points in therapy, however, the EFT therapist "internalizes" responses. For example, rather than asking for a description of a husband's withdrawal and how it affects him in his life, as a narrative therapist might do, the therapist will ask in the here and now how it feels to withdraw and what happens when he does this. The EFT therapist will then ask the wife how she feels when her husband withdraws. As the experience of withdrawal is expanded, new experiences and expressions arise that modify the withdrawer's position. The couple is not engaged in EFT, in a process of fighting bad habits, as narrative therapists help couples to do (Zimmerman & Dickerson, 1993), but in reprocessing experience and expressing new aspects of that experience in such a way as to undermine the problematic pattern. This then allows partners to experience alternative ways of being with their spouse.

EFT and narrative approaches also focus on the ongoing creation of identity. Narrative writers often speak of what the problem has told people about themselves or what identity the problem has talked them into. EFT therapists, on the other hand, listen for the self-definition that emerges in emotional experience and help the person articulate it. They attempt to expand this sense of self through new emotional experiences and new interactions with the most significant "audience" of all, the other spouse.

There are also times when stories and narratives are deliberately used by the EFT therapist. These are:

- When the therapist summarizes and creates brief "stories" of each partner's attachment history as it relates to present interactions. The therapist uses the story to validate and legitimize the person's present perceptions and responses. This is done in front of the other spouse and places this partner's behavior in the context of his/her attachment history, often allowing the spouse to see his/her behavior as a reflection of this history, rather than simply a response to the present relationship. The more insecure the person's attachment style, the more inconsistent and incoherent his/her story about self in relation to others tends to be (Main & Goldwyn, in press). The therapist has then to support these clients more in the construction of their attachment story.

- A disquisition (described more fully in Chapter 3) is an intervention in which the therapist tells the couple a story about couples in general or about a fictional couple similar to themselves. The therapist tells the story of the couple's relationship as he or she understands it, including elements that the couple do not acknowledge, but the therapist conjectures are present. The narrative reflects the therapist's sense of the couple's present reality in a discursive nonpersonal manner that elaborates on aspects of experience the couple seem to want to avoid or cannot articulate. This intervention is less transparent and more indirect than other EFT interventions. The partners usually identify with some aspect of the story and begin to talk about their own experience in the light of the story. The aim of this intervention is to expand the partners' experience in the least threatening way possible or to suggest an alternative way of understanding the relationship.

- Later in the therapy process, the therapist and the couple construct the story of the therapy. This story summarizes the process the couple have been through and the changes they have made. This can be done to consolidate such changes or to highlight an impasse. As partners formulate and refine this story, crystallizing key change events and their part in creating them, the story becomes more integrated and creates a new model for the relationship, which the couple takes with them when they leave therapy.

How does EFT differ from the narrative approach? The most striking difference is that EFT focuses upon emotional experience and the creation of new emotional experience in the session. This new emotional experience can then be integrated into a new story of the relationship. *The focus is less on the cognitive account/description of experience and more on the experience itself. Rather than attempting to "name the alternative plot" (White, 1993), the EFT therapist attempts to create it and have the partners experience and enact it in the session.*

So questions such as, "What actions would you be committing yourself to, if you were to more fully embrace this knowledge of who you are?" (White, p. 46, 1993) are replaced in EFT by a focus on the person's immediate emotional experience and an enactment of new behaviors that expand the sense of self, as in the following:

EXAMPLE

Therapist: What happens to you when your wife says this?

Husband: I get mad, but I stay silent.

Therapist: What is it like for you, to get mad and stay silent?

Husband: It's hard, I'd like to say, (*pause*) but I get anxious.

Therapist: It's scary, but you'd like to say . . . ?

Husband: Get off my back. Stop berating me.

Here, the therapist's focus on the emotional response evokes the action tendency implicit in the angry emotion. When the husband allows himself to feel and express his anger, he knows what he wants and that is to set some limits for his spouse. He is then able to enact this in the session, and begin to create a new "plot" for interactions with his wife.

In EFT, experience and enactment tend to come before the synthesis of a new story. This is logical since EFT assumes that emotional experience is the key element in attachment "plots." As Bruner (1986) suggests, there are always feelings and lived experience not encompassed by a person's dominant story or, in EFT terms, by a person's current awareness. The vulnerability of withdrawn partners, for example, is often left out of distressed couples' interactions and accounts of their relationship. EFT evokes such experience in the session and thus challenges the way the couple makes sense of their relationship.

The narrative therapist might ask a partner to reflect on different elements of their experience, to discuss such elements, and to reason about their habits and beliefs in the light of this experience, for example, to identify and discuss unique outcomes. These are times when the problem did not occur or was handled differently. The EFT therapist is more likely *to create unique outcomes in the session* or to heighten and expand those that occur naturally than to discuss those that have occurred in the past or in other contexts. Strong negative affect also tends to predispose couples to discount and distrust unique responses from their partner. This makes such responses difficult to repeat, unless they occur in therapy where the therapist can support them.

EFT, perhaps, has more of the quality of a drama rather than a narrative. From an attachment point of view, if working models are taken as similar to a narrative or a set of stories of relatedness, it may be difficult to expand such models/narratives without using emotionally oriented interventions to access such core cognitions and to evoke a corrective emotional experience.

EFT and Solution-Focused Approaches

With regard to the solution-focused approach, it is easier to identify the differences between this approach and EFT than the similarities, apart from the general parallel of both approaches sharing a constructivist and nonpathologizing orientation. Whenever possible, the EFT therapist also talks about and heightens and elaborates on what is going on right now between the couple, how they made that happen, and what such events mean for their relationship; however, to propose an extreme dichotomy, as some solution-focused therapists have done, between a solution and a problem orientation omits the focus of experiential approaches—the person. *EFT is neither solution nor problem oriented, but person oriented.* In experiential approaches, the person is always seen as larger than the problem and as having the "solution" to the problem.

The alternative to being solution focused is, then, not necessarily to be immersed in the problematic, dominant story (Friedman, 1992), provided the therapist takes the stance that the person's personhood and experience are larger than the problem and the story of the problem. Immersion in experience does not, as some solution-focused therapists have suggested (Friedman & Langer, 1991), mire client and therapist in pathological thinking. In fact, immersion in experience, particularly emotional experience, is a direct road to new ways of seeing, new emotional responses, and new relationship stories. The person, from the experiential point of view, is overwhelmed not by a problem story, but by his/her way of processing experience and enacting the drama of attachment relationships.

From the EFT perspective, focusing only on exceptions to the problem is likely to discount the partners' pain and the significance of their struggle. In attachment contexts, negative emotion can become such an absorbing state that it is difficult to access meaningful exceptions or to get partners to trust them and accept them as legitimate. This is particularly true if such exceptions open the floodgates of hope and fear, rendering the person vulnerable again to loss and disappointment. If a focus on exceptions does not work, then the solution-focused therapist might ask questions, such as asking a wife how she might respond differently to her husband if his "spiteful" behavior was due to hurt feelings. From the EFT vantage point, such insights or changes in perspective are more easily entertained when the wife has seen her husband experiencing hurt and when he has expressed this experience to her and also when a therapist can help her process this. The EFT therapist would initiate this process and encourage the wife to respond differently in the here and now of the session. This new experience then becomes a key element in a new story of who her husband is and who he can be in relation to her.

EFT and New Behavioral Approaches

In addition to the solution-focused and normative approaches, new versions of traditional approaches are emerging. For example, behavioral therapists have recently begun to integrate experiential interventions, that focus on emotional experience and the creation of acceptance between the partners (Koerner & Jacobson, 1994). In these interventions, the therapist encourages the expression of feelings that are likely to foster compassionate responses from the partner; the problem can then become an opportunity for an intimate conversation, a chance to make contact. This version of behavioral marital therapy, influenced as it is by experiential concepts, focuses upon the pattern of interactions and emotional experience more than traditional behavioral approaches. Its originators make the point, however, that there is less emotional exploration and intrapersonal discovery than typically occurs in EFT. They speak instead about changing the stimulus control in the interaction; that is, changing how one partner expresses him/

herself—in order to change the other partner's response to a more accepting one.

If they cannot be solved by traditional behavioral methods, problems can then be accepted and become less destructive to the relationship. A discussion of when such acceptance is possible can be found elsewhere (Johnson & Greenberg, 1994). It may be that such acceptance is possible only when the behavior that is to be accepted, rather than changed, does not constitute an attachment threat. For example, distance in certain specific situations might be accepted, whereas promiscuity might not. This work extends the behavioral troubleshooting intervention, which does address emotional responses. However, from an EFT viewpoint, this technique tends to label emotional responses and to focus exclusively on their effects, rather than engaging in a reprocessing of such responses. In brief, this approach seems like an *outside in* approach to change, rather than an *inside out* approach, such as EFT.

SUMMARY

Traumatic experience is not traumatic simply because it is described that way (White, 1993), and attachment separation and loss are traumatic. Generally, the EFT perspective is that grief and fear cannot be "solved" or discussed out of existence. They can, however, be encountered in such a way as to evoke adaptive responses that enhance a partner's sense of self and the possibility of nurturing contact with intimate others. Focusing on such emotional responses is not seen as "enlarging the client's view of the problem and intensifying his distress" (Friedman, p. 299, 1992), but as helping this person integrate such responses into his/her sense of self and relationship in a way that expands experience and generates new meaning frames. The EFT perspective is that new meaning and new behavior most powerfully arise from reprocessing experience with the therapist as a guide, rather than from a discussion of such experience. New labels and new ideas are seen as less powerful than new experience here, particularly experience that enhances a couple's ability to engage emotionally.

The strength of all these new approaches is that they add to the growing tendency in marital therapy to make therapy a relatively brief and respectful collaboration, where couples' resources are validated and their problems are seen as part of the human condition rather than a reflection of personal deficits.

10

APPLYING EMOTIONALLY FOCUSED INTERVENTIONS IN A FAMILY CONTEXT

The conviction that human beings have a need for connection with and confirmation from members of their family has been inherent in approaches to family therapy from the very beginning. However, family therapists usually focus on what occurs *between* individuals; emotions, viewed as occurring *within* individuals, are most often not addressed. Although there have been exceptions (Liddle, Dakof, & Diamond, 1991), emotional responses have usually been considered unimportant or even subversive to systemic theory and therapeutic practice (Krause, 1993).

To a therapist who views emotion as a primary link between the biological and the social, the self and the system (Johnson & Greenberg, 1994, 1995), this seems unfortunate. Emotional experience and expression play a large part in organizing and regulating social interactions in families and can also play a significant part in reorganizing such interactions in therapy. Including emotionally focused change strategies in family therapy would address the concerns of authors who have suggested that current family therapies, focusing as

they do on the conversational metaphor, neglect the experiential and the need for clients to experience themselves and their
situation differently (Chang, 1993).

BASIC GOALS AND TECHNIQUES

This chapter is a relatively brief outline of the use of emotionally focused experiential techniques with families. The focus
of this book is couples therapy. However, since the perspective
and techniques elaborated for couples here are also applicable
to other family relationships, this chapter presents them in
this context. The assumptions, goals, and processes of family
therapy using emotionally focused interventions are essentially the same as in EFT. The therapist accesses key emotional
responses that underlie the interaction patterns that define
family relationships, particularly the relationship between the
Identified Patient/Client (IP) and the parents. As in EFT, the
therapist uses new emotional experience and expression to
modify such patterns. The assumption is that if such relationships change for the better, then the IP's problematic behaviors
will also change and this process will also impact how the IP
is defined in the family and in his/her own inner world. The
relational position of the IP in the family is viewed as helping
to maintain this person's problems and/or prevent adaptation
and change.

*The goal here is to modify family relationships in the direc-
tion of increased accessibility and responsiveness, thus helping the family to create a secure base for children to grow in
and leave from.* From an attachment point of view, the more
secure the relationships an adolescent has with his/her attachment figures, the easier it is for this person to act independ-
ently and to confidently explore his/her environment. Secure
attachment is characterized by the capacity to maintain close
supportive relationships while also creating and maintaining
personal autonomy. It is also associated with the ability to
deal with environmental stressors and improved emotional
adjustment, perhaps because secure connections with others

tend to have a positive effect on the psychological factors such as self-efficacy (Bartholomew & Horowitz, 1991; Mikulincer, Florian, & Wester, 1993).

Format

In this kind of family therapy, the general treatment format is that the family is seen all together for the first one or two sessions. This is to assess interactional positions and patterns and to identify problematic relationships and family cycles that appear to be related to the symptomology of the IP. After these sessions, family subsystems are invited to the following sessions: typically, the parents/couple, the sibling subsystem, the IP and each parent, and the IP and both parents. This treatment involves a flexible combination of dyadic, triadic, and family group sessions.

The process of using the expression of newly processed emotions to create new interactions is essentially the same whether the session involves a client dyad or triad. However, dyadic sessions often encourage a sense of safety and focus that allows for the creation of increased emotional engagement when this is desired. Changes made in the dyadic sessions are integrated in triadic sessions into the triangle of IP and both parents. Treatment is designed to take 10 to 15 sessions and to be implemented by a single therapist or two co-therapists. Treatment usually ends with a session where all the family members are present.

Prerequisites and Contraindications

The prerequisite for this kind of family therapy is that the therapist be able to join with the family and individual members and to gain the families' trust and confidence, so that members actively engage in the therapy process.

This kind of intervention is not appropriate for abusive or violent families since the expression of vulnerability and a certain openness is fostered as part of the treatment process. Not only is this difficult to achieve in violent relationships but it may even be inappropriate or put members at physical risk.

Also, this kind of treatment may not be appropriate for families whose members now live very separate lives and who do not wish to examine or improve the contact between members.

FIRST SESSIONS (1–2)

These sessions combine treatment and assessment. The assessment focuses on:

- How family interactions are organized in the session—that is, who speaks, who is allied with whom, and who is excluded; how fixed the boundaries of various alliances are; how predictable and rigid the interactional patterns are in general; who is the most dominant and in control in the family; what strategies do members use to deal with conflict and the frustration of needs. How members respond to requests for support and comfort? Have particular events or crises occurred recently, or in the past, that seem to crystallize the way the family interacts and that they then enact as they talk about the event?
- What is the emotional tone of the family in the session? What kinds of emotions are expressed and by whom? Who seems to be in pain in the family and how do they contain or express it? What are the family expectations about how emotions are dealt with? How do members respond to each other in the session?
- How are patterns of accessibility and responsiveness perceived by the members of the family and how do they hamper or help in the developmental tasks facing the family at this point in time?
- What is the family's story? How did they get to therapy and what do they want from therapy? What is the attachment history of the couple and the manner in which the family evolved to its present state, including how crises occurred and how the problem evolved from various

members' points of view. How do different members perceive the nature of the problem, right now? How is responsibility for the problem assigned?

- What is the contract for therapy? How does the family view the therapy process? Can the therapist connect with the members and the family as a whole? How ready are individual members to engage in the therapy process—for example, to consider suggestions and to agree to try tasks set by the therapist in the session?

By the end of the assessment, the therapist should be able to identify key problematic cycles of interaction and to hypothesize about how they help to maintain the symptoms of the IP. The therapist also should be able to identify key relationships where attachment is problematic, and to have some sense of the emotional responses that prime interactional patterns. A clear sense then emerges of how relationships might be reorganized and attachment needs and fears addressed.

WORKING THROUGH SESSIONS

These sessions, which involve various family dyads and triads, involve the same steps that have been identified in EFT in the working through phase. They are:

- Accessing the unacknowledged feelings underlying interactional positions.
- Reframing the problem in terms of underlying feelings, attachment needs, and interactional patterns.
- Promoting identification with disowned needs and aspects of self and integrating them into relationship interactions.
- Promoting the acceptance of others' experience and new interactional responses.
- Facilitating the expression of needs and wants and creating emotional engagement.

As in EFT, these steps may describe the process in one session or across sessions and are often cycled through more than once, with different levels of engagement. To illustrate this part of the family therapy process, a case example and then a typical session from such a case follow.

CASE EXAMPLE OF EFFT

The family consisted of a very traditional father, a mother, and three adolescent daughters. The oldest daughter was depressed and bulimic; she had dropped out of college. Father was highly educated and came from an ethnic background of extreme poverty and distant family relationships.

The father was seen as critical, controlling, and inaccessible by his wife and daughters, who all expressed anger at his habitual criticalness. He justified his actions in a rational, painstaking, logical manner, stating that he was helping them. They dismissed and ignored his arguments. Mother portrayed the marriage as empty and lonely, and alternated between blaming her husband for all the family problems and taking them upon herself. She then would become very weepy and upset, and threaten to leave. The daughters all seemed careful around the parents, but they were visibly angry with the father.

The family pattern was that Father would criticize and lecture, Mother would try to intervene, with no effect, and everyone would become very angry with Father. Mother would then become hysterical and say that everyone was driving her crazy and she was leaving the family. One of the girls would then get hysterical or sick and the family would calm down. Mother did occasionally leave the house during this sequence, but only for a few hours. After a short period of calm, the cycle would begin again. Overconcern and overprotectiveness coexisted in the family with a lack of contact (no one in the family ever touched the others) and security.

The oldest daughter, in particular, was trying to deal with her father's criticism and contagious fear of failure, as well as her mother's depression, and need for support from her daughter. She had gone away to college, but she was terrified of leaving her mother lonely and depressed, and terrified that her parents would separate or that she would disappoint them by failing. After six months of college, she had become suicidal and bulimic and returned home. To move out of this family and have a more separate life meant, for this young woman, facing all her fears of failing and thereby shaming her father and her family, as well as the possible loss of and betrayal of her mother.

Sessions were held with the family, the couple (who presented as a dominant withdrawer (husband) and a depressed, enraged pursuer (wife), the siblings, and the IP and each parent. By the end of therapy, the IP was in control of her bulimia and depression, and she had moved out to live with a friend. She had also applied to go back to college. The mother had begun to grieve the loss of her role as mother and to confront and rebuild her "empty" life. She was deliberately less obsessed with her children's success and less worried about them. She had taken steps not to intrude into the IP's life and she had begun to reengage her husband in a marital relationship, as well as to formulate some goals for her own life. The sisters were also closer and more supportive of each other. The father seemed to accept his wife as more of an equal in the marriage and to understand that his "worrying" and "advice-giving" behavior resulted in his family keeping him at a distance. He subsequently became more accessible to both his wife and daughters.

A Typical Session

What might one session of emotionally focused family therapy (EFFT) look like, with the family described above?

In a session with father and daughter (Session 5), the therapist introduced the topic of the apparent distance between them. The father said that he was upset by this distance. The therapist helped him to expand and heighten this and to express his sense of loss to his daughter. With the therapist's help, his daughter told her father that he drove her away with his critical lectures and constant advice about how she should be if she was to be "successful." They then enacted their usual dance, with the father justifying his advice giving and blaming his daughter for not listening, while she withdrew.

The therapist helped the daughter to access the compelling sense of sadness and helplessness that arose for her in this situation and to express this to her father. The daughter explored her sense that in this relationship she was defined as a failure and a disappointment. The therapist helped her to articulate how this undermined her confidence and resulted in her spending most of her time warding off and running away from the overwhelming panic that this evoked.

The therapist supported the father to stay focused in the dialogue and to respond directly to his daughter. The daughter went on to tell him how much she needed his approval (a Step 7 process). She also told him how desperate she was when she shut him out, and that she withdrew to protect herself and to avoid the panic she had described previously. The therapist then framed the father as trying to protect and give to his daughter by his advice-giving, examining how this strategy unfortunately left both of them feeling helpless and afraid—he, because his daughter did not "listen" to his warnings, and she, because her father had "no faith in her."

Both were portrayed as the creators and victims of the cycle of critical advice-giving and silent withdrawal. The father then stated that he did not know how to get close to his daughter or how to be a "good father." The therapist suggested that in this family the daughter was the "expert" in showing warmth and approval and could perhaps help her father with this. He agreed that he would like to learn. The therapist also framed the father's approval as the key that could help the daughter manage her anxiety about going out into the world. The father, who had been marginalized in this family, was moved and encouraged by this frame, which was designed to act as an antidote to his sense of isolation and powerlessness, and to his resulting coercive style. In this session, the father and daughter found a way to "unlatch" from their usual pattern of interaction and create a new, emotionally engaged dialogue. At the end of the session, they were primed to begin to turn to each other way to regulate their fears and anxieties, rather than triggering these fears. The daughter was also established as an expert in closeness, who could help the father learn about this; as a result, she moved into a more equal and more adult relationship with him. This session reorganized the participants' interaction and this, in turn, impacted the family unit: It moved the father closer to his daughter and gave the daughter another potential source of support. The mother was then able to give up her mediator role, and to begin to change the nature of her involvement with the daughter.

This session involved a micro version of the process that occurs across many sessions in EFT. The goal here was to begin to modify the father's critical way of engaging with his daughter, since this seemed to be associated with her eating disorder and suicidal behaviors, and to foster interactions with him that would increase her sense of efficacy.

INTERVENTIONS USED IN THIS SESSION

Reflection of Experience

EXAMPLE

Therapist: So, help me understand here, when your daughter called you and told you she was going skiing for the weekend, her first weekend at the university, you felt this tightness, this tension. You felt you had to warn her that spending weekends this way might result in her failing. Is that right?

Reflection of Pattern

EXAMPLE

Therapist: What just happened here? Marsha, your dad was telling you how he says these things for your own good, to protect you, and you turned your head, and then your whole body, away from him.

Marsha: I tune him out. I don't have to listen to this.

Therapist: Ah-ha, he's trying to protect you, and you're trying to protect you from him, from what you hear in his voice?

Marsha: Right. I hear, I'm going to blow it, I'll never make it, and anyway he knows what will make me happy better than I do.

Therapist: So you get angry. Is that okay? (*Marsha nods.*) You tune him out, and then you (*to father*) get even more tense and try harder to get her to hear you; you push more. Is that it? (*He nods.*)

Validation

EXAMPLE

1. **Therapist:** So Marsha, when you left home you carried this weight on your back. Here you were going out into the world, which can be pretty terrifying just in itself, but you were also worried sick (*This is a deliberate frame, as she was bulimic.*) that you would fail to please your parents, let the family down, let yourself down by failing to meet your "potential," right? (*Marsha nods.*) Also, you were worried that, without you there to talk to, Mom would become more and more depressed, and then she might leave and the family would fall apart. Incredible weight to carry, so hard, I'm amazed that you made it through a whole term.

EXAMPLE

2. **Therapist:** It's so so important for you, Tom, to be a good father, to try to be, as you put it, the perfect dad. That's lots of pressure. And if Marsha starts to have difficulties,

it sends you a message that you are deficient here. You should be able to prevent such things, yes?

Evocative Responding

EXAMPLE

1. **Therapist:** What is it like for you, Tom, to hear that your daughter becomes paralyzed by fear if she lets herself listen to your warnings and "lessons"?

EXAMPLE

2. **Therapist:** What happens for you, Tom, when your daughter talks of how much she needs your trust, needs you to believe in her, to approve of her?

Heightening

EXAMPLES

Therapist: Can you tell him again, Marsha, can you tell him, "I'm a disappointment to you, I know I am."

Therapist: So, can you tell her again, Tom, "I'm so afraid for you. It's so hard for me to see you walk out into the world, away from my roof, my shelter, and face the world that nearly destroyed me when I was young." Can you tell her, please.

Empathic Conjecture

EXAMPLE

Therapist: And with all this pressure, Marsha, you get worried sick, yes? (*She nods.*) You try not to eat, to be slimmer, and to feel more in control. Then you get very hungry and scared and eat lots of food to comfort yourself. Yes? (*She nods.*) But then you feel even more worried. It's like, you have lost control. You have failed, and all the weight of disappointing Dad and leaving Mom comes flooding in and you throw up. Is that it, have I got it right?

Reframing

EXAMPLE

Therapist: So, it's hard to get a hold of your fear and let your daughter find her own feet out there, Tom? It's hard just because she is so precious, yes? And because you feel your duty, as a good Dad, is to protect her. For you, Marsha, all the warnings feed your own fears and part of you just gives up, gets paralyzed, yeah? Except when you get really angry at Dad and decide to stop trying, to kind of spite him, is that it?

Restructuring Interactions

EXAMPLE

Therapist: So can you tell him, Marsha, if I can try and summarize what you just said, "I need to know that I'm special to you and that you think that I can do it, that I can fly on my own. And that even if I crash, I need to know that everyone will survive and I'll still be special to you, even if I quit school." Is that it?

TERMINATION SESSIONS

In these sessions, the focus is on highlighting changes from old patterns and responses, heightening the families' strengths and sense of self-efficacy, summarizing treatment gains, consolidating new interactional patterns, and supporting the family to formulate new solutions to old problems. Treatment ends with a family session with everyone present, where the collective family story of the problem, the therapy, and the present status of the family are summarized.

DIFFERENCES FROM EFT

In EFFT, there is a more intense focus on modifying specific interactions that appear to contribute to the IP's difficulties, with less focus, even in the couple sessions, on building intimacy per se. In the couple sessions, for example, the focus is on how the couple can help each other support the identified patient and actively create the kind of family life that they desire. Thus, the focus is more circumscribed than in EFT: It is the couple's relationship, as it influences the larger system of the family. For example, the mother might describe how she turns to her oldest daughter for help when she perceives her husband as unavailable. The session might then evolve around how each parent views the consequences of this for the oldest daughter, for the other siblings, and for the marital relationship, as well as addressing the blocks to emotional engagement between the partners.

Couple sessions might also focus on how the problems of the IP have impacted the parents' relationship and come between them as a couple. For example, when a wife accuses her husband of being ineffectual in tackling their daughter's problem, the therapist supports the husband to challenge his wife's viewpoint. He then is able to tell her how he would like to take care of his daughter and her, if only she will let go of the reins a little. He goes on to suggest that this would also allow the wife to step back from her power struggle with her daughter.

The couple are addressed as the architects of the family, not simply in terms of their own relationship. The EFFT therapist still attempts to increase safe emotional engagement between the couple and thus to improve marital satisfaction, but *the primary goal is to modify the interactional position of the IP in relation to the other members of the family*. If the couple wishes to focus more intensely on their own relationship, they may request couple sessions after family treatment has terminated.

The end of EFFT is usually characterized not by a softening of the more hostile spouse as in EFT, but by new responses on the part of the identified patient. These responses typically take the form of more assertive boundary definitions, including definitions of self, more clearly expressed attachment needs, and a more active definition of the relationship that he/she desires with other members of the family. It is often the case that EFFT helps adolescents go through attachment separation, or at least the redefinition of the attachment relationship between parents and adolescent into a more adult and secure form, where difference and separateness can be tolerated. In many families, the children have to first connect before they can effectively leave.

In addition to the interventions used in EFT, this form of family therapy uses the assignment of some tasks and rituals to be completed outside of the therapy session. For example, the therapist might suggest that the siblings share an activity each week and so enhance the relationship between them. Structural systemic interventions have traditionally included the setting of such tasks (Minuchin & Fishman, 1981), but they have not been used in the EFT format. However, in EFFT as well as in EFT, change is still generally viewed as occurring within the session rather than outside it.

If two therapists are involved with the family (EFFT is often, but not always, conducted with two therapists), then an intervention can occur where the two therapists enter into a brief dialogue with each other about the family or the nature of the interactions happening in the session. This is similar to a reflecting team type of intervention in that the family members become an audience witnessing a conversation that focuses on them and their relationships. In EFFT, however, this is usually a very brief discussion that is used for a specific purpose, rather than being a general and/or widely used intervention. It is, in fact, often a form of validation and/or conjecture, presented in a dialogue format. For example, one therapist might say to the other, "You know, I'm not sure I understand what is happening here, do you?" The other replies, "Well, I'm not quite clear whether Sarah (*the daughter*) is pleading for some acceptance from her Mom, or if she is more interested in showing her Mom that her Mom can't control her, that Sarah can push her buttons by simply eating a large bag of potato crisps." The therapists then turn to the family for clarification. This is done only when the session seems stalled in an impasse or when the family is very reactive and emotionally volatile. For a moment, it turns the family into an audience rather than participants and introduces a more distant perspective for their consideration.

PRESENT STATUS OF EFFT

At present, EFFT has not been systematically, empirically validated, but a pilot project is in progress to address this issue. It has also been applied systematically only to families where adolescents (between 14 and 19), are struggling with depression and/or eating disorders. It arose out of the realization that the change principles and strategies used in EFT could be applied to different contexts and different relationships—that is, to change interactions between father and daughter, as well those that occur between marital partners, and that changing such relationships then modified problematic family cycles of interaction.

This kind of family therapy addresses the concerns of those who are disturbed by "the disappearance of the individual into a systemic stew" (Merkel & Searight, 1992, p. 38) and attempts to extend systems theory by looking both within and between.

11

THE PEANUT BUTTER INCIDENT: AN EFT SESSION

Husband: I tried to kiss you this morning, and you rejected me.

Wife: I had my mouth full of peanut butter at the time.
I said, hold on, I'm busy.

Husband: So, I'm less important than peanut butter.

A professional couple in their late forties came to the marital and family clinic in a large urban hospital. Their names were Paul and Elsa, and they had been married for 20 years. They had two children approaching adolescence. At their assessment, they appeared to be a relatively sophisticated couple. Paul spoke in very intellectual terms with reasoned arguments and long digressions, while Elsa wept. They stated their problem in terms of lack of intimacy. Elsa stated that Paul was a "stranger" to her and that she had given up trying to be close because she could "never do anything right, no matter what I try." Paul stated that for him the relationship was in the "deep freeze." He was aware that he "pushed" for closeness, which was very much missing for him in the relationship, although he was also aware that he was a "workaholic" who spent most of his life deeply involved in his projects. Elsa stated that she felt continually analyzed and criticized and now avoided Paul by almost any means possible. Paul suggested that he was basically angry because Elsa had "never turned up for this relationship."

This couple's interaction followed a classic pursue/attack and withdraw/avoid pattern, with Paul being the pursuer and Elsa being the withdrawer. The couple were still relatively committed to the relationship, although each of them spoke of the possibility that it would end if things did not improve. Paul suggested that he might leave to find a more responsive partner, while Elsa spoke of leaving to avoid Paul's "constant criticism." At the beginning of therapy, the couple scored 82 on the Dyadic Adjustment Scale (Spanier, 1976). A score of approximately 100 is the cutoff point for marital distress on this commonly used measure; a score of 70 is typical of divorcing couples.

In this chapter, a transcript of Session 11 is presented, together with comments on therapist interventions. This session is an example of how one incident can provide the structure for several sessions of therapy and be used as a microscope to explore crucial aspects of the couple's negative interaction pattern and underlying emotions. The episode presented here, the peanut butter incident, was used in sessions 10 and 11 to access and expand Paul's experience of the relationship and to initiate the softening change event (as described in Chapter 7) with him. This incident was chosen as a focus by the therapist because it vividly captured the responses that characterized key problematic interactions between the partners. It also clearly reflected the nature of the partner's attachment issues. The couple also completed an Interpersonal Process Recall (IPR) procedure (Elliot, 1984), immediately following this particular session, as part of a pilot study for a research project. In this procedure each partner views a videotape of the session with a researcher, who asks questions designed to elicit how this partner experienced the session. This chapter also contains a brief synopsis of these comments.

Before the session presented here, the couple had formed an excellent alliance with the therapist. The first few sessions, however, were challenging in that Elsa would weep and become very silent, while Paul would spin "fogs" (Elsa's label) out of words, taking the session into intellectual, tangential dead ends. The therapist finally suggested that, since she (the therapist) was becoming very confused, she would touch the end of Paul's shoe when this occurred. (He habitually placed one leg across his knee, so his shoe was easily accessible.) This would remind him to slow his mind down and allow the "fog" to clear a little.

In these earlier sessions the pursue/withdraw cycle went through a process of deescalation and the couple began to spend some positive time together. Elsa also became much more engaged in the relationship. She was able to articulate her perception that she had been abandoned for Paul's work early in the relationship, and that now he was like "some stranger who suddenly demands love and intimacy." She was also able to access and express her fear of Paul's criticism. As she experienced it, he was the judge and she was the criminal who was inevitably "condemned." She began to assert her needs in the relationship and to tell Paul that she was not going to be "destroyed" by his "fogs and arrows." She stated that she was not going to give, if her gifts were held up for judgment and labeled "inappropriate" (as was her Valentine's day card).

In session 10, the therapist began to focus upon accessing the insecurity that seemed to prime Paul's constant monitoring of Elsa's behavior and his critical analysis of that behavior. At this time, the couple recounted the peanut butter incident. This incident, where Paul had tried to make affectionate contact with Elsa, was for him an example of her "unattainability." It had occurred the day after their anniversary, which they had spent together in a relatively close way, but which had then resulted in a reinitiation of the negative cycle. In this incident, Paul had tried to kiss Elsa when she was eating peanut butter, but he was "rebuffed." He then spent the whole day fuming and delving into dark, pessimistic scenarios about the relationship and about the impossibility of connecting with anyone. Elsa, on the other hand, felt "coerced and trapped" and she withdrew, although to a lesser extent than previous occasions. Session 10 ended with Paul accessing some of his hurt and fear, but accusing Elsa of being unresponsive and withholding.

Elsa became disoriented when Paul began to talk of his fears of being rebuffed, asking "Who are we talking about?" The therapist suggested that Elsa found it difficult to see Paul's sensitivity and pick up his attachment signals because she was not prepared for such messages from a partner whom she saw as a "dangerous judge." She also suggested that Elsa did not understand these signals because Paul presented them "in disguise," as humorous and unimportant, to lessen the risk inherent in asking Elsa for a response. Let us now look at Session 11.

SESSION 11

Elsa: I wouldn't know how to describe this last week.

Paul: We had a bit of a tussle yesterday morning.

Elsa: We get off track. We need to know how to stay on track.

Paul: What is on track?

Elsa: When it's calm.

Therapist: Is "on track" the same as what happened on your anniversary, when you were together, and, Elsa, you felt close and, Paul, you felt that Elsa was "attainable?"

Paul: Yeah, but she's attainable such a small percentage of the time. Most of the time we're in neutral. There are high points, but then it's cut off, and then there's strong disagreements.

Therapist: Is it like you were talking about last time, Paul, on the anniversary, you had a great day together. And then the next morning you went to Elsa and asked her for a kiss, and her mouth was full, and you felt rebuffed. Then that broke the spell for you. There are moments when you are together, connected, and then something happens to break the spell, yes?

Therapist creates focus by bringing in the incident, described in the last session, that interrupted a positive experience and reinitiated the negative cycle.

Paul: Yeah, there is this habit we're in. It can be strong, like a whack. The other day, I tried to pinch your bum and you whacked me really hard (*to Elsa*).

Elsa: I thought you were playing.

Therapist: So this is the same. Something good is happening and you (*to Paul*) want to carry it on. You reach for Elsa somehow, and if she's not right there, right at that moment?

Paul: Yeah, I can detect a certain level. It's like she says, "I'll give you a squeeze," and then, "Oh, time's up. It's time to move onto something else." I'm very much, I'm a little starved, and so for me it's like, heh, this is the beginning not the end.

Therapist: You're hungry. You're starved. You want the contact and then, for you, it gets cut off.

Reflection. Evocative responding using Paul's image of deprivation.

Paul: Yeah, there's no question it gets cut off. Clearly, that is what happens. I'm not working in her space in the right way to get beyond that.

Elsa: I don't live it the way you do. I don't see it this way.

Therapist: Well, in the last session (*to Paul*) we talked about you being hungry and that you have an incredible sensitivity, and when you reach for Elsa at these times, it's like having what you want just for a moment and then losing it. Then you go off and say to yourself, "There you are, she's never going to connect with me. There you are, no one is ever going to connect with me." It becomes a catastrophe. Remember that stuff?

Reflection. Heightening.

Paul: Yeah, that's it. I drag it out into the atomic bomb, and at an emotional level, that's what I'm feeling. Even when it's a joke, like we make it into a joke, both of us, there is something inside us that says, this is no joke.

Therapist: It's not a joke. It's a bomb.

Paul: Yeah, but if she decides . . . .

Therapist: It's like last time, where you talked about playing the game and Elsa making the rules?

Paul: Oh, since day one. It's like Charlie Brown and the football; that's my complaint, whether it's valid or not, but you (*to Elsa*) feel like I set the rules (*Elsa nods.*) Well, *you* set the timetable in terms of intimacy.

Therapist: And suddenly you feel cut off.

Evocative responding, focusing on the experience of loss.

Paul: Yeah, it happens so often that, you're right, I'm hypersensitive to it.

Therapist: Elsa, you're looking puzzled, like in the last session, and I remember last session you said to Paul, "What are you talking about?"

Paul is in Step 5 here, while Elsa is trying to accept his new responses, that is she is moving into Step 6 of the therapy process.

Elsa: Yeah, Russian.

Therapist: You said to Paul, you're talking in Russian. Right, it's like, "I don't see this vulnerable person?" (*Elsa agrees.*) You see the person who sets the rules, the judge, the critic. You described it to me once as, "I see fog and arrows."

Reflection of Elsa's experience of Paul.

Elsa: I don't remember saying that, but I like it.

Therapist: I'm hearing that you have been so busy here, protecting yourself from Paul's criticisms, from being "devastated" (*Elsa's word*), that for you to actually now get a sense of the fact that this dangerous critical person is in fact incredibly vulnerable and hungry for contact with you . . . .

Elsa: Yeah, it doesn't add up.

Paul: I'm setting myself up here. She's content and I'm hunting around.

Therapist: (*to Paul*) Could you tell her what's going on at those times? Could you say, "I feel hurt. I wanted a kiss and you said no?" (*Paul pulls his head back and raises his eyebrows.*) You couldn't tell her?

Paul: It's obvious in the action. I put my arm around her.

Therapist: So she should know, know that you are trying to get some reassurance from her. Is that word alright for you, "reassurance"?

Interpretation/Conjecture.

Paul: Reassurance, acceptance. If she's attractive and I want to be close, and I do it. It's devastating to try, and oops, it doesn't work.

Therapist: It's devastating to reach, and you can't get her to respond.

Reflection.

Paul: Yeah, the response is a joke. (*He looks sad, near tears.*)

Therapist: It's not a joke, is it Paul? Because these times all add up to a sense that you're never going to get your needs met here. It's deadly serious, right? All these little wounds add up to something deadly serious.

Heightening . . . Conjecture.

Paul: Yeah, if Elsa laughs at me, and my melodrama, I laugh too. She pricks my balloons and I admire that in a sense.

Therapist: Some part of you says, "Oh okay, she's pricking my balloon, isn't that funny. But another part doesn't think it's funny at all?"

Therapist continues the heightening.

Paul: Not at all.

Therapist: The urbane scientist part of Paul would say, "Oh isn't that funny, she's just pricked my balloon." Then this other part would feel just devastated. This vulnerable side of Paul, that starts to feel that he's going to go hungry his whole life, that he's never going to be able to reach Elsa, to keep hold of that connection with her, is devastated.

Reflection and Heightening. The therapist heightens the attachment significance of his experience.

Paul: Yeah, that's the problem, from my perspective anyway. You said it well.

Elsa: What balloon, what do I prick?

Paul: Maybe I'm blowing something up. I inflate this kind of incident into something big.

Therapist: (*to Elsa*) The way I understand it, the balloon is what happened on the anniversary day. It's when you two get together and Paul, you start to feel, my god, we're together, my god, this is it. She likes me. I'm connected, she is with me, here we are, it's happening. And there is this *hope*, this precious tenuous feeling of connectedness, and the next day you go to pat her on the bum or to kiss her, and if she doesn't respond, if she says, my mouth's full or anything (*pause*) . . . .

Heightening. Interpretation. Conjecture. The therapist evokes an attachment drama of hope and loss. The therapist also pauses to invite Paul to continue in this frame.

Paul: Yeah (*to Elsa*), like the other day. I just reached for your hand in the car, and you pulled away, like I was a hot poker, you know?

Paul brings up another example of these incidents. This whole dialogue creates a new position for Paul in the relationship, which replaces his original detached, judgmental stance.

Elsa: No, no, no, what was happening was . . . (*to therapist*). But finish the bit about the balloon.

Therapist: The sense I have is, that you feel close and it's good. The balloon is this incredible sense of hope, that you two are going to be together, and Paul will have his hunger for closeness satisfied.

Paul: And then, it doesn't happen.

Therapist: And then it gets BURST. Do you understand (*to Elsa*)?

Elsa: I guess I do. It's difficult for me to see why my mouth being full of peanut butter and saying, just a second, is piercing a balloon.

Paul: Yeah, but after that the dance doesn't continue. The play changes. It's going in a different direction afterwards.

Therapist: Yeah. We did talk about that. The sense I get is that you both recognized these incidents the minute they happen. What you (*to Elsa*) said was (*in session 10*), "The minute I turn him down, I look at his face and I know he doesn't like it, and he's tense, and I know I've blown it. He's mad at me, and I feel trapped and so I withdraw," right? (*Elsa agrees.*) And you (*to Paul*), say to yourself, "There you are, you see, it happened again. I'm not going to do this anymore." And as you drive to work, this grows into, "This will never work, she will never be there." So something happens in that moment and the two of you back off like mad. And you, Elsa, say, "He's pushing me, I've got to kiss him or he'll be mad," and,

Paul, you say, "She wasn't available for long, she's shut me out again."

Therapist paints a picture of this part of the cycle and its attendant emotional responses.

Paul: This is the balloon. In the face of these disappointments, I get into, do I really want the kiss (*angry tone*)?

Paul adds in the anger, the blaming element that dominated his part of the cycle at the beginning of therapy and that pushes Elsa away.

Therapist: If you can never trust that this connection is really going to be there, some part of you says, I'd rather not want it, right? I don't want to want this kiss.

Paul: Yes, it's a confused state, and thoughts and feelings come along that are very destructive and very judgmental and condemning. Like, you can keep your damn kisses.

Therapist: You can keep your damn kisses. Some part of you wants to say to Elsa, if you're going to suddenly shut me out, you can keep them, I don't want them, keep your kisses. (*All laugh.*)

Reflection and Heightening. The therapist heightens this because it places Paul's hostile behavior in an attachment frame of disappointment and insecurity.

Elsa: All because of a mouthful of peanut butter.

Paul: No, so many thousand instances, you know. This was just one.

Elsa: You know, (*to therapist*), we were driving and he was trying to get my hand, you know, like a little guy, maybe going to hold his girlfriend's hand. So I moved it a quarter of an inch, and he couldn't grab it and I laughed. But he was so kidlike, so, I thought, he's playing. But now I realize, maybe he was not playing. I was the only one who was playing!

Paul: I wasn't playing! I'm not playing at all. I'm trying to get a message across at these points when I come to you. You can characterize them as kidlike. When it comes to these things, I'm just not good at it. When I do make these little gestures and it appears funny to you, it might appear funny, but it's not funny.

Therapist: (*Soft voice*) Aha, it's not funny. It's you taking a risk and saying, are you still there? Do you still desire me? Tell me again, because I need to know that I'm really special to you. It's you doing that, right?

Conjecture using an attachment framework.

Paul: (*tears*) Yeah. She does let me know sometimes. Last week, in the market, she said, "I'd still pick you out of a crowd," and that made me feel good.

At this point, the therapist would normally ask Paul to tell Elsa that he needs reassurance that he is special to her and that he is very afraid that he is not. This is consciously not done here because in previous sessions this task proved to be excruciatingly difficult for Paul and would result in many intellectual digressions. The therapist, therefore, chooses to keep the present focus and initiate this intervention at a later date.

Therapist: You're a very intellectual person, Paul, but when you reach for Elsa at these times, it's a physical reaching. And it might look small, insignificant, playful, but in fact, its serious. A serious attempt to find out if she's still there. (*Paul nods.*) And if, for whatever reason, she isn't, and there might be incredibly good reasons, like your mouth is full (*all giggle*), somehow that bursts the balloon, dampens the hope, puts things back in neutral or worse.

Paul: I am so sensitive. I know that sometimes Elsa can't do any right, you know. In bed this morning (*to Elsa*), you were trying to get extra space, maybe you were still asleep, and I made a move like that (*to touch her*) and you swatted me, like a fly, you know. I interpret that as rejection and I get angry.

Again the therapist chooses not to get Paul to express his feelings and needs directly to Elsa, but instead dramatizes his anger herself.

Therapist: (*To Elsa*) Keep your kisses. (*Paul nods.*) What's happening Elsa, what's happening as Paul is talking about this?

Therapist switches focus to the other partner, to keep her engaged and facilitate her Step 6 process.

Elsa: I was trying to understand. But when I say nice things, it doesn't count. It was the wrong place or the wrong time. I think we both do it to both of us. He doesn't take it when I do tell him nice things. It's always the wrong time.

Therapist: So, for you, there are times when you reach out to give, and Paul doesn't take what you have to offer?

Elsa: That's it. (*Puts her hands up in front of her in a gesture of apparent helplessness.*)

Paul: It did make me feel good, when you said that, about picking me out in a crowd, but I do qualify it. I guess, I put it in context. The context of all the other times she doesn't want to be there, that she prefers the TV or the dog.

Elsa: As soon as you qualify something, you don't take it as it is.

Paul: Well, it's when I'm vulnerable and we are alone that I want you to say those things, but I did like what you said when we were in the market, in a crowd.

Elsa: (*Agitated*) Well, if you think that, when we are in bed, that I'm going to roll over and say take me, I'm yours, this isn't me. On this planet I'll never do this, this isn't me.

He qualifies her giving by saying that it occurred in the wrong place. This is the trigger for Elsa's irritation. She states her unwillingness to be controlled by Paul and his demands, which she had also asserted in earlier sessions.

At this point, however, it seemed like a detour, so the therapist moved to contain the detour. It is also a potentially negative stance here, where Elsa defines herself as someone who cannot or will not respond to Paul's needs, just as Paul is struggling to express them in a new way.

Therapist: I'm confused. I remember in session 5 or 6 that you told Paul, I do want to give myself to you. Do you remember that? (*She nods.*) And you said, "I try, and you don't accept my offer." So I have heard you say to Paul, I want to be with you.

The therapist wants Elsa to stay engaged at this point.

Elsa: Yes, I do, but not in this form, this, take me, I'm yours, form.

Paul: It's not the form I care about, it's not the form. If I put my arm around you, I just want to be close to you. I just want you to respond.

Therapist decides to redirect the session.

Therapist: Let's go back to the mouthful of peanut butter. I like that one.

Elsa: (*Laughs*) Yeh, you love that one.

Therapist: Yeah. I liked it. Elsa you said that you were busy, and Paul you said to Elsa, you pay attention to the dog when you're busy, do you remember? (*Paul laughs.*) It feels like a clear example of these incidents we are talking about. When you feel safer, you aren't feeling like Paul is about to judge you so much, you can be close, and Paul you feel that she is there. Like she wants you. Kind of the opposite to what you said once, when you said that she'd never turned up for this relationship. You connect, and then Paul you need to reassure yourself that you really did touch that closeness. You reach to find her again, to reassure yourself that it was real, right? (*Both nod.*) And the timing is a little off, and, Elsa, you can't quite respond in that moment, and then, Paul, you're devastated, and the two of you withdraw and that negative cycle starts.

Conjecture built into a drama.

Paul: Yeah, and it's happening at a really subtle level.

Therapist: Right. But what isn't subtle is that then that negative pattern sets in. Paul you get angry and critical, and Elsa you shut him out and withdraw. So these little incidents throw all that good sense of connection off again.

Tracking and Reflecting the cycle as it appears here.

Elsa: It sounds danger again.

Therapist: Right. Yeah, right. The alarm goes off again. It has been safe for a while and suddenly the alarm goes off. And then, Elsa, you say, "I'll never do it right, why try," and, Paul, you say, "I didn't want her kisses anyway," and get angry.

Paul: Yeah, we're laughing a little about it now, we can see it now, but when it happens . . . (*turns to Elsa*) I notice you don't cry so much in these sessions now.

Elsa: Well, the sessions are not so difficult.

Therapist: Yeah, in the first sessions, Elsa, you talked about your pain in the relationship, but then you came out and drew some lines about Paul's criticism, but now (*to Paul*) we are talking about your hurts in the relationship.

Paul: I'm still critical now. I'm no different.

Therapist: Feels pretty different to me.

Elsa: It's not as negative, the tone is different.

Paul: I'm still complaining, but maybe with less voltage.

Elsa: It's not like it used to be. If it happens, I can ignore it now.

Paul: Why would you do that?

Therapist decides to refocus the session again from what seems like a detour initiated by Paul.

Therapist: The relationship is safer for you (*to Elsa, who nods*)? Now we are talking about when you, Paul, feel vulnerable in this relationship. When you are out there, searching for this reassurance, that's hard.

Paul: Yeah, it's a much harder topic for me. That's for sure.

Therapist: It's hard for you to talk about that?

Paul: Elsa can open up, she can emote.

Therapist: It's harder for you to show Elsa the emotional side of you. (*Paul nods*) So it would be really hard for you in those situations that prick the balloon to let Elsa know how devastated you feel when you cannot reach her again. To show the part that gets hungry and scared that you've lost her again, and that for you she's gone back to being unattainable.

Repetition of attachment themes.

Paul: (*Very still and quiet*) She sees that.

At this point the therapist again chooses not to ask him to tell Elsa how hard it is for him to be vulnerable with her.

Therapist: Does she? In the last session she said quite clearly that she didn't see it.

Elsa: I never saw it this way. I always saw it as a joke.

Paul: I speak in irony, with humor, that's my style.

Elsa: When you reached like that, it was so clumsy, it couldn't have been any clumsier, honest to God.

Paul: Maybe I present it as a joke.

Therapist: (*Reflectively, slowly*) It was clumsy. Paul is a very sophisticated person, the opposite of clumsy. Suddenly, here is this different person, suddenly he is clumsy, and you say to yourself, "This is a joke." (*Elsa nods.*) But it is not a joke, is it Paul? Most of us, if we get scared and we are right on the edge of the cliff and facing something we long for very much and are scared that we are never going to grasp, we don't look cool and sophisticated. We fumble, we miss, we don't read the clues right. We get clumsy, we are so terrified that what we want so much is not going to happen.

Validation, Heightening. A brief general conjecture to provide a context for Paul's behavior.

Elsa: (*To Paul*) I didn't see it like that.

Therapist: There is no reason why you should see it. You are used to seeing Paul as this super competent scientist, this powerful person. Perhaps you are not prepared for this other side of Paul. (*She nods.*) And Paul, in the last session you talked very movingly about how Elsa is still beautiful for you. (*He nods.*) You talked for a moment in the voice of a young man who has just fallen in love, who might be clumsy. I guess, I am struck by this word clumsy. At these points when you're reaching for Elsa, you're not cool and in control. You are the Paul who is vulnerable, more unsure of yourself, reaching for something you're not sure is there? (*Paul agrees.*) And Elsa, you look, and you see urbane Paul, who can shoot you down with a single arrow, and you say to yourself, "Oh, he is joking." (*Elsa nods.*)

Therapist uses the word clumsy to heighten the sense of Paul's vulnerability.

Paul: Under these clumsy moments there is a real fear. A fear that this is all going to fall apart. Maybe it was never solid, maybe the connection was never there, and why don't I just accept that. It's loaded.

This is the first time that Paul has openly acknowledged fear.

Therapist: Maybe it was never there?

Paul: Yeah, maybe it was an illusion. My little gestures are ways of saying, hey, let's not go down that path.

Therapist: The path that leads to the loss of the relationship, right?

Paul: Right. But maybe, maybe, it's too needy that part. It's not attractive, there are attractive and unattractive elements . . .

The therapist notes this and will go back to this in the next session. What the therapist hears here is the working model of self—in this case, a model of the dependent self defined as unlovable. This arises very frequently at this point in the process. For now, however, the therapist decides to refocus the session.

Therapist: So what are you trying to say to Elsa when you reach for her, Paul? You're trying to say . . . ?

Now the therapist invites him to take the risk and express his need.

Paul: (*Long pause, laughs*) Let's get married!!!!! (*Elsa laughs.*)

Therapist: Let's get married. So, in that little touch is, "Let's get married." Come and be with me, or, are you going to be with me or not? (*Paul smiles and nods.*) It's a proposal in disguise. It's done in a way that you're not so naked, so vulnerable, yes?

Therapist heightens Paul's response and accepts the level of risk he is ready for at this time.

Paul: So when she doesn't respond, when I don't get reassured, it's like I'm less important than peanut butter.

At the end of the session the therapist validates how Paul is taking risks and how Elsa is struggling to see, as she puts it, a "brand new Paul." She then ends the session by talking about how strong and how sensitive they both are and how much impact they have on each other. The therapist's goal for the next session was then to continue the softening process, and to request that Paul state his fears and needs directly to

Elsa. This would then move him into Step 7 of the therapy process. In contrast to the first few sessions, Paul brings more and more of himself into the interaction and is more and more accessible, and Elsa is engaged and available.

Couple Process

After this session, each partner was shown a videotape of the session and encouraged to comment on the process. This was done with the understanding that partner's comments would be shared only with the researcher and not with the other partner or the therapist. Such sharing only occurred later, when the couple agreed to allow the information to be used in this volume. The interviewer asked process-oriented questions, such as, "What was happening for you here?" Both partners assessed the session as productive, assigning it an eight on a 10-point scale, and both explicitly stated that they trusted the process of therapy, even if they were not always clear as to where it was going, and they trusted the therapist.

Paul's Perspective

Paul commented that the therapist put "her finger on how he was feeling. She tuned into me." He particularly noted that it moved him when the therapist recognized how vulnerable he was. Paul felt dismayed when his wife stated that she did not see the vulnerable side of him and sensed that the therapist was emphasizing this to help Elsa see it.

Paul wanted Elsa to be more involved in the session, to say more instead of "hesitating," because, as he stated, "the only thing that really counts is Elsa's reassurance to me that she wants to be with me. I need to hear that from her." As well as recalling how he experienced the session at the time, when he watched the video he stated that he could observe himself "bullying the relationship" and "playing a negative record" by criticizing Elsa. He stated that this probably set things up not to work.

Elsa's Perspective

Elsa thought that the session was a good one because she was hearing things from Paul that she had never heard before, and this was "very revealing." She felt that they were "discovering things that were buried. We are on the right path." She also experienced Paul as less blaming and accusing in this session. She saw him as taking a risk and "being scared of my reactions, that I might think he was a wimp." She suggested that, "If we keep going this way, I'll understand better and I'll be there better. As opposed to being in a fog, being lost, and shutting him out." For Elsa, Paul's speedy, intellectual, and ever changing comments and asides often confused and overwhelmed her to the point where she would just stop listening. In this session, the "fog had lifted."

Elsa also stated that she didn't want to say too much in the session and interrupt the process of Paul expressing himself. She wanted to give him space and hear what he had to say, so she stayed quiet. She felt that the session had been not only "an eye-opener, but an ear-opener." Even though she was quiet, she felt included in the session. She recognized that in the first sessions she had often been the focus of attention and she had felt "understood" by the therapist, and that now it was Paul's turn. Elsa mentioned that she felt good when the therapist redirected the session after her comment "to say, take me I'm yours, that is just not me." She felt that this comment was a "dead end." She also felt "put on the spot" by Paul here and felt like resisting his pressure. Paul, on the other hand, felt a little cut off here by the therapist, but commented that if he had kept going in this vein Elsa would probably have "frozen" on him.

In the next session, Session 12, Paul talked more openly about how his vigilance and monitoring of Elsa's responses reflected his "fear," specifically the fear of losing the relationship. He also spoke of his sense of being "invisible" and not having an impact on Elsa. Elsa responded that she could not read his mind and was "bound to fail" if he could not show himself more. The therapist suggested he help Elsa with this and Paul spoke of his anxiety about showing his vulnerability to Elsa, because she might "jump all over him." At the end of the session he stated, "It's fearful for me to feel how much I need you, to feel my dependence. That I can sing in the shower or not because of you, that my happiness relies on your acceptance." He then asked her, "Do you really feel okay about me being dependent and needing reassurance?" Elsa told him that this was not a problem for her, although she still felt a little hesitant, because she still viewed him as "a little dangerous."

Session 12 continued the process of the softening which Paul began in session 10 and continued in the session transcribed above. In these sessions, Paul moved between Steps 5 and 7 of the EFT process, while Elsa moved slowly and surely through Step 6, accepting new aspects of Paul and coming to trust them. Every couple is different and this couple were very aware (even before the IPR procedure) of the process of therapy. In previous sessions, Paul had sometimes asked the therapist, "What are you doing here?" The therapist would then tell him. For example, the therapist at one point replied, "I am blocking your exits and trying to slow you down, so you can stay right here, in this place for a while, because I think that right here is very important." The process of therapy was, therefore, more transparent than usual because the couple wanted it that way.

Later in therapy, Paul was able to talk openly about his "deep longing" for closeness with Elsa and a sense of being "wanted" by her. Elsa was then able to respond positively to this. She attributed her increased engagement in, and satisfaction with, the relationship to the fact that she now "had more of a voice here," and she could "stand up more." At the end of therapy this couple scored 107 on the Dyadic Adjustment Scale, placing them in the nondistressed range on this instrument.

EPILOGUE

This practical guide to EFT is written in the hope that it will contribute to the evolving field of marital and family therapy. It was written for beginning therapists, one of whom once told me, "I know how to touch people's emotions, but I don't know what to do with them once I get there." It is my hope that such therapists will, after reading this book, have a clear sense of how to access and shape emotions, and of how to use them to change interactions in intimate relationships. This book was also written for more seasoned therapists who, hopefully, might find EFT useful and incorporate its techniques into their own wisdom and style. It was also written for me, in that the writing of such a book forces any therapist to articulate what it is that he/she does know and to struggle with what he/she does not know, and so to learn more about the art of therapy.

Like the field of marital therapy, EFT is still evolving and the couples I see continue to teach me how to connect with them and how to help them strengthen and expand their relationships. However, there are also two general concepts that, as I see more and more couples, seem more and more salient to me. The first is the power of validation. To be seen and affirmed, first by the therapist and then by one's partner, is often a very powerful change event in and of itself. It is also an intervention that is one of the basic building blocks of the experiential therapies. The use of such affirmation requires that the therapist adopt a nonpathologizing stance, one that implies trust in the client's intentions and abilities. More than this, the therapist has to be able and willing to be a student of, rather than an expert on, how particular individuals construct their experience.

Second, although many years ago Alexander (1948) spoke of the need for a corrective emotional experience in therapy, it seems as if this concept has taken very much of a back seat to skills training, cognitive insight, and behavior change in the predominant, popular models of marital and family therapy. The focus has been on rational rather than emotional processes. To me, it makes ultimate sense that when one employs therapy modalities that focus on the most powerful emotional bonds we ever make, new emotional experience is a primary, direct, and particularly salient route to change, and to the forging of new emotional connections with others. The power of tapping into emotional processes and using them to shape interactional positions still surprises and enthralls me. In EFT, this corrective emotional experience, where each partner interacts with the other in a new way, not only reorganizes negative cycles, but is often able to foster a more secure and loving bond between partners. In many cases, therapy then ends, not only with an alleviation of symptoms, but with the initiation of a new and vibrant intimate connection.

REFERENCES

Alexander, F. (1948). *Fundamentals of Psychoanalysis*. New York: Norton.

Alexander, J. F., Holtzworth-Munroe, A., & Jameson, P. (1994). The process and outcome of marital and family therapy: Research review and evaluation. In A. Bergin & S. Garfield (Eds.), *Handbook of psychotherapy and behavior change* (pp. 595–607). New York: Wiley.

Bartholomew, K., & Horowitz, L. (1991). Attachment styles among young adults. *Journal of Personality and Social Psychology, 61*, 226–244.

Berger, P., & Luckmann, T. (1979). *The social construction of reality*. Harmondsworth, England: Penguin Books.

Bowlby, J. (1969). *Attachment and loss: Vol. 1. Attachment*. New York: Basic Books.

Bowlby, J. (1988). *A secure base*. New York: Basic Books.

Bretherton, I. (1990). Open communication and internal working models: Their role in the development of attachment relationships. In R. Dienstbier & R. Thompson (Eds.), *Socioemotional development: Nebraska Symposium on Motivation* (pp. 57–114). Lincoln, NE: University of Nebraska Press.

Bruner, J. (1986). *Actual minds, possible worlds*. Cambridge, MA: Harvard University Press.

Bruner, J. (1990). *Acts of Meaning*. Cambridge, MA: Harvard University Press.

Burman, B., & Margolin, G. (1992). Analysis of the association between marital relationships and health problems: An interactional perspective. *Psychological Bulletin, 112*, 39–63.

Chang, J. (1993). Commentary. In S. Gilligan & R. Price (Eds.), *Therapeutic conversations* (pp. 304–306). New York: W.W. Norton.

Christensen, A., & Heavey, C. L. (1990). Gender and social structure in the demand/withdraw pattern of marital conflict. *Journal of Personality and Social Psychology, 59*, 73–81.

Dandeneau, M., & Johnson, S. M. (1994). Facilitating intimacy: A comparative outcome study of emotionally focused and cognitive interventions. *Journal of Marital and Family Therapy, 20*, 17–33.

Dessaulles, A. (1991). *The treatment of clinical depression in the context of marital distress.* Unpublished doctoral dissertation, University of Ottawa, Ottawa, Canada.

Dunn, R. L., & Schwebel, A. I. (1995). Meta-analytic review of marital therapy outcome research. *Journal of Family Psychology, 9*, 58–68.

Elliott, R. (1984). A discovery-oriented approach to significant events in psychotherapy: Interpersonal process recall and comprehensive process analysis. In L. Rice & L. S. Greenberg (Eds.), *Patterns of change* (pp. 249–286), New York: Guilford Press.

Fisher, L., Nakell, L. L., Terry Howard, E., & Ransom, D. C. (1992). The California Family Health Project: III. *Family Emotion Management and Adult Health Family Process, 31*, 269–287.

Friedman, S. (1992). Constructing solutions (stories) in brief family therapy. In S. H. Budman, M. F. Hoyt & S. Friedman (Eds.), *The first session in brief therapy* (pp. 282–305). New York: Guilford Press.

Friedman, S., & Langer, M. T. (1991). *Expanding therapeutic possibilities*. Lexington, MA.: Lexington Books.

Gottman, J. M. (1979). *Marital interaction: Experimental investigations*. New York: Academic Press.

Gottman, J. M. (1991). Predicting the longitudinal course of marriages. *Journal of Marital and Family Therapy, 17*, 3–7.

Gottman, J. M. (1994). An agenda for marital therapy. In S. M. Johnson & L. S. Greenberg (Eds.), *The heart of the matter:*

Perspectives on emotion in marital therapy (pp. 256–296). New York: Brunner/Mazel.

Greenberg, L. S., Ford, C., Alden, L., & Johnson, S. M. (1993). Change processes in emotionally focused therapy. *Journal of Consulting and Clinical Psychology, 61*, 78–84.

Greenberg, L. S., James, P., & Conry, R. (1988). Reviewed change processes in emotionally focused couples therapy. *Family Psychology, 2*, 4–23.

Greenberg, L. S., & Johnson, S. (1985). Emotionally focused therapy: An affective systemic approach. In N. S. Jacobson & A. S Gurman (Eds.), *Handbook of Clinical and Marital Therapy* New York: Guilford Press.

Greenberg, L. S., & Johnson, S. M. (1988). *Emotionally focused therapy for couples.* New York: Guilford Press.

Greenberg, L., Rice, L., & Elliott, R. (1993). *Facilitating emotional change: The moment-by-moment process.* New York: Guilford Press.

Greenberg, L. S., & Safran, J. D. (1987). *Emotion in psychotherapy: Affect and cognition in the process of change.* New York: Guilford Press.

Guerney, B. G. (1994). The role of emotion in relationship enhancement marital/family therapy. In S. M. Johnson & L. S. Greenberg (Eds.), *The heart of the matter: Perspectives on emotion in marital therapy* (pp. 124–150). New York: Brunner/Mazel.

Guidano, V. F. (1991). Affective change events in a cognitive therapy system approach. In J. D. Safran & L. S. Greenberg (Eds.), *Emotion, psychotherapy, and change* (pp. 50–82). New York: Guilford Press.

Gurman, A. S. (1992). Integrative marital therapy. In S. H. Budman, M. F. Hoy, & S. Friedman (Eds.), *The first session in brief therapy* (pp. 186–203). New York: Guilford Press.

Hazan, C., & Shaver, P. (1987). Conceptualizing romantic love as an attachment process. *Journal of Personality and Social Psychology, 52*, 511–524.

Hazan, C., & Shaver, P. (1994). Attachment as an organizational framework for research on close relationships: Target article. *Psychological Inquiry, 5*, 1–22.

Hofer, M. A. (1984). Relationships as regulators: A psychobiologic perspective on bereavement. *Psychosomatic Medicine, 46*, 183–197.

Izard, C. E, (1977). *Human emotions.* New York: Plenum.

Jacobson, N. S., & Addis, M. E. (1993). Research on couples and couples therapy: What do we know? Where are we going? *Journal of Consulting and Clinical Psychology, 61,* 85–93.

Jacobson, N. S., Follette, W. C., & Pagel, M. (1986). Predicting who will benefit from behavioral marital therapy. *Journal of Consulting and Clinical Psychology, 54* (4), 518–522.

Jacobson, N. S., Holtzworth-Munroe, A., & Schmaling, K. B. (1989). Marital therapy and spouse involvement in the treatment of depression, agoraphobia, and alcoholism. *Journal of Consulting and Clinical Psychology, 57,* 5–10.

Jacobson, N. S., & Margolin, G. (1979). *Marital therapy: Strategies based on social learning and behavior exchange principles.* New York: Brunner/Mazel.

James, P. (1991). Effects of a communication training component added to an emotionally focused couples therapy. *Journal of Marital and Family Therapy, 17,* 263–276.

Johnson, S. M. (1993). *Healing broken bonds.* A marital therapy training video. Department of Psychiatry, Ottawa Civic Hospital, 737 Parkdale Avenue, Ottawa, Ontario, K1Y 1J8, Canada.

Johnson, S. M., & Greenberg, L. S. (1985). The differential effects of experiential and problem solving interventions in resolving marital conflicts. *Journal of Consulting and Clinical Psychology, 53,* 175–184.

Johnson, S. M., & Greenberg, L. S. (1988). Relating process to outcome in marital therapy. *Journal of Marital and Family Therapy, 14,* 175–183.

Johnson, S. M., & Greenberg, L. S. (1992). Emotionally focused therapy: Restructuring attachment. In S. H. Budman, M. F. Hoyt, & S. Friedman (Eds.), *The first session in brief therapy* (pp. 204–224). New York: Guilford Press.

Johnson, S. M., & Greenberg, L. S. (Eds.). (1994). *The heart of the matter: Perspectives on emotion in marital therapy.* New York: Brunner/Mazel.

Johnson, S. M., & Greenberg, L. S. (1995). The emotionally focused approach to problems in adult attachment. In N. S. Jacobson & A. S. Gurman (Eds.), *Clinical handbook of marital therapy (2nd ed.)* (pp. 121–141). New York: Guilford Press.

Johnson, S. M., Greenberg, L. S., & Schlindler, D. (1996). *The effects of emotionally focused marital therapy: A meta-analysis.* Manuscript in preparation.

Johnson, S. M., & Talitman, E. (in press). Predictors of success in emotionally focused marital therapy. *Journal of Marital and Family Therapy.*

Johnson, S. M., & Williams-Keeler, L. (1996). *Creating healing relationships for traumatized couples: The use of emotionally focused marital therapy.* Manuscript in preparation.

Jordan, J. V., Kaplan, A. G., Miller, J. B., Stiver, I. P., & Surrey, J. L. (1991). *Women's growth in connection: Writings from the Stone Centre.* New York: Guilford Press.

Kempler, W. (1981). *Experiential psychotherapy within families.* New York: Brunner/Mazel.

Kiecolt-Glaser, J. K., Fisher, L. D., Ogrocki, P., Stout, J. C., Speicher, C. E., & Glaser, R. (1987). Marital quality, marital disruption, and immune function. *Psychosomatic Medicine, 49,* 13–34.

Kobak, R., Ruckdeschel, K., & Hazan, C. (1994). From symptom to signal: an attachment view of emotion in marital therapy. In S. M. Johnson, & L. S. Greenberg (Eds.), *The heart of the matter: Perspectives on emotion in marital therapy,* (pp. 46–74). New York: Brunner/Mazel.

Koerner, K., & Jacobson, N. S. (1994). Emotion and behavioral couple therapy. In S. M. Johnson & L. S. Greenberg (Eds.), *The heart of the matter: Perspectives on emotions in marital therapy* (pp. 207–226). New York: Brunner/Mazel.

Krause, I. (1993). Family therapy and anthropology: A case for emotions. *Journal of Family Therapy, 15,* 35–56.

Lazarus, R. S., & Lazarus, B. N. (1994). *Passion and reason.* New York: Oxford University Press.

Liddle, H., Dakof, G., & Diamond, G. (1991). Multidimensional family therapy with adolescent substance abuse. In E. Kaufman & P. Kaufman (Eds.), *Family therapy with drug and alcohol abuse* (pp. 120–178). Boston: Allyn & Bacon.

Mahoney, M. J. (1991). *Human change processes: The scientific foundations of psychotherapy.* New York: Basic Books.

Main, M., & Goldwyn, R. (in press). Interview-based adult attachment classifications: Related to infant–mother and infant–father attachment. *Developmental Psychology.*

Merkel, W. T., & Searight, H. R. (1992). Why families are not like swamps, solar systems or thermostats: Some limits of systems theory as applied to family therapy. *Contemporary Family Therapy, 14,* 33–50.

Mikulincer, M., Florian, V., Wesler, A. (1993). Attachment styles, coping strategies and post traumatic psychological distress. *Journal of Personality and Social Psychology, 64,* 817–826.

Minuchin, S., & Fishman, H. C. (1981). *Family therapy techniques.* Cambridge, MA: Harvard University Press.

Minuchin, S., & Nichols, M. (1993). *Family healing: Tales of hope and renewal from family therapy. New York: Touchstone Books.*

O'Hanlon, B., & Wilk, J. (1987). *Shifting contexts: The generation of effective psychotherapy.* New York: Guilford Press.

Pennebaker, J. W. (1990). *Opening up: The healing power of confiding in others.* New York: Avon Books.

Pierce, R. A. (1994). Helping couples make authentic emotional contact. In S. M. Johnson, and L. S. Greenberg, (Eds.), *The Heart of the Matter: Perspectives on emotion in marital therapy* (pp. 75–107). New York: Brunner/Mazel.

Plutchik, R. (1980). *Emotion: A psycho-evolutionary synthesis.* New York: Harper & Row.

Roberts, L. J., & Krokoff, L. J. (1990). A time-series analysis of withdrawal, hostility, and displeasure in satisfied and dissatisfied marriages. *Journal of Marriage and the Family, 52,* 95–105.

Roberts, T. W. (1992). Sexual attraction and romantic love: Forgotten variables in marital therapy. *Journal of Marital and Family Therapy, 18,* 357–364.

Rogers, C. (1951). *Client-centered therapy.* Boston: Houghton-Mifflin.

Snyder, D. K., & Wills, R. M. (1989). Behavioral versus insight oriented–marital therapy: Effects on individual and interspousal functioning. *Journal of Consulting and Clinical Psychology, 57,* 39–46.

Spanier, G. (1976). Measuring dyadic adjustment. *Journal of Marriage and Family, 13,* 113–126.

Sternberg, R. J., & Barnes, M. L. (1988). *The psychology of love.* New Haven: Yale University Press.

Walker, J., Johnson, S., Manion, I., & Cloutier, P. (in press). An emotionally focused marital intervention for couples with chronically ill children. *Journal of Consulting and Clinical Psychology.*

Walker, J. G., & Manion, I. (1996). *Emotionally focused marital therapy: A two-year follow-up study.* Manuscript in preparation.

Watzlawick, P., Weakland, J. H., & Fisch, R. (1974). *Change: Principles of problem formation and problem resolution.* New York: W.W. Norton.

White, M. (1993). Deconstruction and therapy. In S. Gilligan & R. Price (Eds.), *Therapeutic conversations* (pp. 22–61). New York: W.W. Norton.

White, M., & Epston, D. (1990). *Narrative means to therapeutic ends.* New York: W.W. Norton.

Wile, D. (1981). *Couples therapy: A nontraditional approach.* New York: Wiley.

Wile, D. B. (1994). The ego-analytic approach to emotion in couples therapy. In S. M. Johnson & L. S. Greenberg, *The heart of the matter: Perspectives on emotion in marital therapy.* (pp. 27–45). New York: Brunner/Mazel.

Yalom, I. D. (1980). *Existential psychotherapy.* New York: Basic Books.

Zimmerman, J. L., & Dickerson, V. C. (1993). Bringing forth the restraining influence of pattern in couples therapy. In S. Gilligan & R. Price, *Therapeutic conversations* (pp. 197–214). New York: W.W. Norton.

NAME INDEX

SUBJECT INDEX